Voices of C

Christians:

Towards the Universal

Janice Dolley

and Heather-Jane Ozanne

First published in Great Britain in 2023 by Sleepy Lion
Publishing.
(Trading name of Sleepy Lion Limited)

Text Copyright © Janice Dolley and Heather-Jane Ozanne,
2023
Cover © Sleepy Lion Publishing 2023
Interior art © Sleepy Lion Publishing, 2023
Editing © Sleepy Lion Publishing, 2023

ISBN: 978-1-8380496-9-0

SLEEPY LION
PUBLISHING

www.sleepylionpublishing.com

CONTENTS

ACKNOWLEDGMENTS

We would like to thank the following people who have helped bring this book to fruition:
First and foremost to the biographers, who have generously shared their stories and whose work forms the heart of this book we offer our heartfelt gratitude.

Thank you to our friends in CANA (Christians Awakening to a New Awareness) who have sponsored this publication and especially: Jane Upchurch www.janeupchurch.co.uk, Rev. Don McGregor www.donmacgregor.co.uk and Judy Hanmer.

To Diarmuid O'Murchu, we are grateful not only for writing the Foreword but for the many years of inspiration he has provided to so many seekers after truth, authenticity, new theological understanding and a more just world.

Finally, we deeply appreciate Michael Amos and Sleepy Lion Publishing for their patience and excellent guidance.

Note from authors: this book has been a collaborative work. Each of us has contributed from our own reflections and understanding, striving to achieve unity in our diversity, (achieved through the heart) to bring about this book. It is our hope that this book will help people in their own journeys of faith, depth, and spirituality.

Janice Dolley and Heather Jane Ozanne

PART ONE

Foreword by Diarmuid O'Murchu

In 2021, the American-based Jesus Seminar (otherwise known as the Westar Institute) published a highly original, albeit controversial, book entitled *After Jesus Before Christianity* (edited by Erin Vearncombe et al.). Based mainly on archaeology and ancient history, it delves deeply into Christian practice covering a period of 250 years from 50-300 CE. This period has been regarded as one of ecclesiastical growth and development into the hierarchical church of later centuries, but the research of this book highlights a very different course of development.

The Christian Church we have come to know over the centuries, built around hierarchical structures, leadership by priests and bishops, doctrines based on authoritative teaching, formal liturgies, and distinctive moral codes, did not begin to emerge until after Constantine made Christianity the formal religion of the Roman Empire during the course of the 4th century (the 300s). Prior to that time, Christianity was very much an informal, highly fluid people's movement, characterised by a great deal of creativity and diversity. And central to that creative unfolding process was the gathering around the table, at a vast range of different meals that also provided the context for much reflection, dialogue, and the working out of values for living, inspired by the prophetic life and ministry of Jesus.

As I read through *Voices of Contemporary Christians*, I kept making connections with what I had read in *After Jesus Before Christianity*. Particularly in the personal stories constituting the bulk of this book, I hear voices of frustration, disappointment, and a deep hunger for a more dialogical and creative way of living the faith whether in a Christian or other religious context. Clearly, what many of these seekers are searching for is a "church" beyond the rigidity, legalism, and over-institutionalisation that emerged during the Christian centuries and is now rapidly declining amid the evolutionary forces characterising our 21st century.

The Waves of Change

The opening chapter of *Voices of Contemporary Christians* highlights the waves of change sweeping through our modern world, and the growing desire for more organic, interactive ways of being, particularly in the search for deeper spiritual meaning. This also includes the desire for a reformed church with a capacity for deeper listening and more meaningful dialogue as expressed in the Catholic church's preparation for the 2023 Roman synod. These are certainly noble and timely aspirations, but all our churches must also become more transparent in dealing with the inherited baggage of imperial power still very prevalent in our time.

And that brings me to another significant book, *In the*

Shadow of the Gods, published in 2022 by Dominic Lieven, Emeritus Professor of History at Cambridge University. Lieven traces the history of kingship going back about 5,000 years, noting how kingship in many parts of the ancient world evolved around the notion of allegiance to the Sky-God considered to be the ruling king of the entire universe. This theme permeates the entire Old Testament, leading to the view that Jesus too must be descended from a royal line if he is to be an authentic messenger from God.

Amazingly, therefore, Lieven never once references kingship in the Old Testament. He never cites the famous monarchical figures of Saul, Solomon, or David and never alludes to Jesus' royal decent from the patriarchs of yore. Why not? Because the actual historical evidence is very shaky and unreliable. And yet the entire Judaeo-Christian tradition is constructed on imperial foundations, which over the centuries have been viewed as literal veracity, and allegiance to faith judged on being loyal obedient servants to a Ruling God whom we have long assumed chose to govern God's people through earthly imperial representatives, namely kings, popes, bishops, etc.

Beyond our Imperial Conditioning

This king-like dispensation is what the anti-global activist, David Korten (in his 2005 book, *The Great Turning*) refers to as 'imperial civilisation,' which he claims is the root and cause of so much destruction, pain, and suffering in our world. It now needs to give way to what he calls an 'ecological civilisation,' in which humans are invited to situate themselves within the evolving web of the whole creation. In several of the personal narratives in *Voices of Contemporary Christians*, people refer to how they grew into deeper spiritual meaning through a rediscovery of nature and the deeper spiritual meaning they encountered in the natural world.

The old imperialism is not merely a threat to our planetary future at a political, economic and ecological level (David Korten's concern), but also a spiritual and theological issue of enormous import. It is our clinging on to divine imperialism and using it as validation for clerical superiority that has resulted in the decline of religion in today's world, and it is impacting all religions to one degree or another. In a sense therefore *Voices of Contemporary Christians* is inviting us all to a post-religious spiritual landscape characterised by a renewed communal spirit of deeper listening, more mutual participation, and empowering dialogue.

Back in the 1970s with the revival of spiritual feminism, the American activist-cum-theologian, Nellie Morton, advocated an empowering strategy of 'hearing people into speech.' When people know they have been heard, when spaces are created for genuine dialogue, when people's real stories of meaning and faith are told without fear or judgement, then the empowerment of the Gospel can arise anew, and a very different world can begin to evolve.

My hope is that *Voices of Contemporary Christians* will be a timely and inspiring contribution to this empowering process.

Introduction: The Landscape of Change

'The times they are a-changing!'[1]

So wrote and sang Bob Dylan and, later in the song, he sounded a note of warning, suggesting there were dangers for those who stall, who are unable to move with the times. Bob Dylan penned these words in the 1960s and they seem equally relevant today, if not more so.

Eric Hoffer, American philosopher, suggested that 'in a world of change, learners shall inherit the earth, while the learned shall find themselves perfectly suited for a world that no longer exists!'[2]

We are living through a time of transition between an era that is passing and a new era that is emerging. There is a huge amount of upheaval and chaos in the world today. It can be challenging and confusing, but this is the context in which we write, and it requires us to learn and consider changes we need to make in response.

It can be tempting to bury one's head in the sand or run for cover, taking refuge in familiar ideas and paths, failing to recognise that they do not address the current global issues and problems. Our approach needs to integrate wisdom from the past with new understandings and discoveries in order to meet the multiple crises in today's world. As Eckhart Tolle suggested, humanity is faced with a stark challenge 'to evolve or die.' If we are unable to create a new world and adapt to it, Dylan further warns that we 'may sink like a stone.'

In 2006, we produced a book titled *Stories of Contemporary Christians: Awakening to a New Awareness.* It addressed many changes that were occurring at that time within Western Christianity. In the decade and a half since then, the speed of change has accelerated and there has been a further erosion of trust just about everywhere, including in our institutions, such as in the medical, political, economic, scientific, and religious spheres. It is probably a rather too well-worn axiom that times of great challenge can also be times of great opportunity. Whilst acknowledging and facing some of the breakdown around us can be daunting, unsettling and disorientating, in this book we look at the signs of possibility and positive change which are emerging, in the world and in Christianity.

So here we begin where we left off all those years ago, with a teaching drawn from the Jewish Tradition called the Four-fold song. The basic idea is that each person needs to be able to harmonise four songs within themselves:

1. The song of self
2. The song of their tribe/s

3. The song of all humanity

4. The song of all life and the whole cosmos.

At the time of writing the previous book, certainly within Christianity, many people were moving beyond previously held boundaries and beginning to connect further than their own tribes of belonging. Now there is an even greater movement towards singing the song of all humanity, the recognition that we are all in this together and that whilst it is important to look out for our own tribe we need to also care and make decisions based on the good of all humanity as well as the planet and all life. A growing number report experiencing a feeling of unifying love flowing throughout the universe, often felt through meditation, prayer or in nature. This experience of love can equate to 'singing the song of all life and the whole cosmos.'

As individuals, communities and nations, we are facing unprecedented times, enormous and discombobulating world circumstances. For many people, the age of reason and the age of certainty have all but disappeared into a soup of relativism and competing worldviews. At every turn, new theories and discoveries challenge dearly held beliefs and our very sense of identity and belonging. In the places and beliefs where we once found security, we now find insecurity, and things we trusted are no longer reliable. Much of the old language doesn't quite resonate and we need to find new language and words to express what is arising within us and in our world.

One small example of this is the word, 'God.' For many, the meaning of this word has changed because contemporary images of who or what God is have changed. Alternative phrases used in recent years include 'the Source of all,' 'the Sacred,' 'the Ground of All Being,' 'Spirit,' or 'Great Spirit.' Rapid change in the world is forcing us to develop new identities, belonging, and beliefs. It is all very complex but when faced rather than hidden from, when we allow ourselves to swim in the tide of change and informed by wisdom, we can arrive at new simplicity – one that allows us to embrace the new. We can integrate past learning, beliefs and identity into a new synthesis, which can propel us forward with the sense of deep of knowing, presence and peace.

In this book, we are presenting aspects of change that many people following a spiritual path, within or informed by Christianity, face. This is in line with the evolutionary shifts of our time, moving in the direction of a more Universal understanding.

It is often in times of change and challenge that we humans dig deeper into ourselves to make sure that our lives are founded on a rock and not built on unstable sand, as the biblical parable teaches. This can then prompt us to question beliefs that have been handed to us by others and that we have not fully taken on board for ourselves. Sometimes this can catalyse an awakening of some kind.

A framework is helpful for us as we progress through life.

A variety of religions and faith traditions have provided this for many people. Political parties or the quest for the American dream have guided others. But as the paradigm underpinning these has fallen away, there is no longer an overarching narrative that helps make sense of all that is going on. As the Catholic priest, Fr. Thomas Berry, said in an essay in 1978:

'We are in trouble…we are in between stories. The Old Story – the account of how the world came to be and how we fit into it – is not functioning properly, and we have not learned the New Story.'[3]

This lack of a shared narrative to guide us and share with future generations means that we are truly living in a time of transition. The global pandemic has shown us that the old story of separation, of adherence to an -ism such as the pursuit of economics at all costs, is being seen to lead us towards a cliff edge as a species.

It is during these times of transition and transformation towards a new normal, or a planetary reboot as some call it, that certain emerging trends will form part of the interweaving threads of a new framework into which our individual lives can fit.

Two millennia ago, Jesus brought good news to the world. He announced through his life, death and resurrection the coming of the Kingdom of God. Yet in many ways this Kingdom, which can also be translated as "reign" or "realm," has an air of mystery about it. One could surmise from Gospel teaching that the Kingdom or realm is both inner and outer, both come and coming

□

and that this realm or Kingdom contains a new vision for humanity, not just for people who are within the institutional church.

Jesus gave the imperative to seek first the Kingdom of God (Matthew 6.8) and to live according to new guidelines. It is not an easy thing to live according to the guidelines he gave us – they call for a change of heart, not merely an outward show of doing the right thing, as well as a move away from judging others. In the Sermon on the Mount and Beatitudes, Jesus sets out a way of living rather than a way of believing. He emphasises humility, peace-making, compassion, and justice. There is now a growing call to go back and re-examine, re-interpret and put into practice in the light of our contemporary world.

The fourteen autobiographical accounts in the next chapter demonstrate a wide variety of ways that people with a Christian background have been discovering the new, emerging story. It seems new to us now but in fact it is also based on ancient ways.

PART TWO

Biographies

Chapter 1: The Importance of our Personal Stories

Biography itself is an important way of arriving at theological and spiritual insight. Journalist Diana Greene writes, 'Biography is inherently theological, that by virtue of the Incarnation every life contains the news of the gospel, that each one of us is a parable.'[1] Drawing on the insight of Kenneth Woodward and Diana Greene further suggests that biography can be a form of primary theology, that each life transformed through faith can be an example of ongoing revelation. Biography is particularly important now, when the former structures of meaning are breaking down and becoming more open; it creates a context that can provide meaning. Many are discovering the importance of hearing the stories of others and telling their own, as a tool of spiritual growth.

Stories, whether biographical, non-fictional or fictional can open us up to deep layers of meaning; they can challenge, inspire and resonate in powerful ways. They are particularly effective because they do not tell us what or how to believe, but place a rich feast before us, the meaning of which is not always immediately obvious but when reflected upon offers insight and wisdom. There is a strong tradition of conveying human and spiritual truths in story and myth, such as in the parables of Jesus, the myriad Sufi stories, and those of many different cultures and indigenous traditions around the world.

Here we are delighted to present the biographies of fourteen people on a path of spirituality and/or faith who would identify themselves as Christian, or post–Christian, or whose spiritual journey has involved Christianity. We are especially grateful to our contributors who have responded with openness and generosity. Each is contributing to the developing awareness of humanity, for we live in times of multiple challenging crises that threaten to destroy life on planet Earth. It is not a set path that lies ahead of us but a call to explore more deeply the mysteries of life and take an active part in the regeneration and renewal that needs to happen before it is too late.

We asked our contributors to focus more on their own experiences rather than produce an intellectual analysis. One reason for this was that we wanted to show that those who may have fled to the margins of the institutional church have not abandoned faith but have come to a different understanding of it, recognising that its essence is universal. Whilst some continue to be active members of their local church, some are unable to find a home within its walls. Others have explored beyond the confines and dogmas of traditional Christian belief and have returned to church attendance but continue to receive, integrate and nurture learning and inspiration from other religious traditions, interfaith dialogue and contemporary spiritual movements.

The biographies have been placed into sections according

to the aspect of change they most reflect, but most of the biographies contain elements of each of the categories.

Voices of Change (Celia and Kate)
Voices of Acceptance (Mary Jo and Janet)
Voices of Discovery (Judy, Sue and Peter)
Voices of Inspiration (Tim and Petra)
Voices of Unity (Jill, Magda and Jane)
Voices of Awakening (Janice and Don)

They were written at different times. Some were for a previous book, *Awakening to A New Awareness: Stories of Contemporary Christians*, published in 2006 by CANA (Christians Awakening to a New Awareness), and these writers have been invited to add a few paragraphs to their original biographies shown as 'Update.' All have moved on from their story we show here, which are snapshots on a moving river. Many of the biographers are or have been affiliated with CANA and refer to it in the accounts of their spiritual journeys.

We hope that you will find enrichment through the following biographies of people who have journeyed in faith, often with courage, open to the challenge of new insights and the inner voice and promptings that birthed change.

Voices of Change

'To live is to change, and to be perfect is to have changed often.'[1]
Cardinal John Henry Newman

In the following two stories, we find a special openness to change, allowing for ongoing shifts that engender an active faith rather than ossification, and which can lead to a continual freshness and willingness to consider new insights.

Celia

It felt like it was in the air. Having brought my children up on Angel's Delight puddings, suddenly everything new and mechanical no longer seemed right. The world appeared to be on a road to disaster. The earth's resources were running out, health was suffering from bad nourishment, and village life was fast declining due to mechanisation, inorganic fertilisers, and imported ingredients. There was a yearning for the "good old days". Communes sprang up where food was grown using little or no mechanical aids, and compost and manure were spread by hand. Vegetarianism became the alternative to battery hens and crated calves and, as awareness grew of horrendous famine in Africa, vegetable protein became a way of increasing the acreage to grow more food. Some of us seemed to be affected by a feeling of urgency that drove us to consider and embrace changes in the way we lived. In our family, we rented some extra land to grow vegetables. Chickens and geese were added though both came to a sticky end and, at a later stage, we had cattle, three steers that became so hungry they escaped into a neighbouring cornfield. I would not give them cattle cake in the winter, as the manufacturers refused to tell me what was in it. I hadn't been so stupid as it turned out when the cause of Mad Cow's Disease became known.

Well, the start of it for me was sometime in the Seventies. We went to a 'real food show' and bought an electric flourmill. A cook by training, I did catering using wholefood ingredients. One thing led to another, and I was giving classes in wholefood and vegetarian cookery. There weren't the recipes in those days, so I made them up, adapted traditional recipes and found how often the base of country food throughout the world was well balanced vegetarian food, rice and lentils, bean stew and dumplings, etc. My family were put through the rigour of roughage. Although we never became vegetarian, most of our meals were without meat or fish. I don't know where the idea came from, there was just an awareness that things weren't right, and we needed to change. It was happening all over; I remember serving a lemon meringue pie made with a wholemeal pastry base at a rather smart luncheon. The Dowager Duchess this and the Lady that swarmed into the kitchen after the meal to ask how I had made it. They had all felt the need to take a step back and use more natural ingredients.

In Spiritual terms, this may not seem very connected, but I believe it was the beginning of my spiritual awakening. No longer could anything be taken for granted, no authority could be trusted, everything had to be questioned and 'the truth' reassessed. Someone came to speak to our Women's Institute about a community in the north of Scotland called Findhorn. My eleven-year-old son was home from school so had to come with me; he was as enthralled as I. My husband agreed, and a month later the three of us and our ten-year-old daughter were on our way for an Experience Week arranged particularly for families. Change? Oh yes it changed us. The Church talks about being born again. I suppose we were 'born again' but it wasn't the Church. It wasn't anti-Christian; in fact, the Christian ethos was very much accepted and, in some cases, practised. However, in our group there were Buddhists, a Hindu, and two Sufis. Together we shared in the community's silent morning and evening meditation. There were no words, or maybe a few at the beginning, and in the stillness no difference applied. In our group sessions, we shared each other's stories, assisted with the work of the community, dug in the garden and played in the trees. We learned to love, to be, and most of all, to trust our intuition.

Meditation became part of our lives, fifteen minutes each morning. When the hall clock struck eight we knew our time was up. No one had taught me how to meditate. I picked it up from books and friends. I would attempt to empty my mind, still it from the jumble of everyday thought. I cannot say how successful I was. Maybe only a minute or two would be achieved, but the effect was to order my life. No matter what was in the day ahead, everything would fall into place and the day would pass without the normal rush and jumble. Sometimes I would feel that another dimension had taken over. It felt so unlike me but was probably the reverse, and I was able to feel the whole me. At the same time, I felt as though I was plugged into the universe. I was aware of the wholeness of life and began to live my life following the path that seemed to open. I learned to trust my impulses, to withdraw if I felt resistance, to push through when the way became clear. We opened our home as a Centre for New Awareness and people came. There was this hunger to learn, to open up our higher selves, to allow thoughts that might have been quashed in the traditional Christian Church.

An opportunity arose to work for an inter-religious group who were organising a conference in India. Circumstances had us in precisely the right position to take on this work. We had a well-equipped office, a computer I could use, a photocopier, and my husband had just taken early retirement. The work took four years with much travel and increasing workload as the conference drew near. We had the opportunity to meet holy people from many different faiths; some gave teaching so pure that it felt like we might have been sitting at the feet of Jesus. Truth lies within the teaching of all the Masters; who can say one is greater than the other?

□

My Christian background is deep and lasting. Regular Sunday worship was in my being from the age of three. I went to a High Church boarding school where the beauty of the Eucharist left a lasting impression. And yet there is so much about the Church that feels alien to the simplicity of that early teacher from Nazareth. I cannot see Jesus as the Son of God any more than I am the daughter of God and 'you and I are one.' I see the Holy Ghost as the life force that is available to us all should we open up to its power and guidance. I cannot stand and profess my faith acknowledging the birth and death of Jesus without giving credence to the power of his teaching and lifetime example. I go to the Christian Church because Jesus is the teacher I best know. The beauty of the service enriches my body, though I need to close my mind to some of the words. The teaching stimulates my thinking, but I would love the opportunity sometimes to question the content; and the community of the Church gives me friendship, but I doubt that many would understand my beliefs.

We have come to know this recent period of time as the dawning of a New Age; a time of great change such as must have happened two thousand years ago when Christianity began. During this last century, psychotherapy has released the constraints of generational straightjackets and given us a deeper understanding of ourselves. Technology has given us the tools for increasing knowledge of humanity and all aspects of creation; and meditation, which seems to be a common factor in all those I know who travel this path, has opened us to realms and

21

experiences we had not previously known. The Church did not always accept the mystics of old, though their language was in Christian terms. Those people I have come to know in the last forty years are using a different language. In their deep experience of meditation, they are meeting, not with Jesus or the Holy Spirit, but are conversing with Guides, higher consciousness, and the higher self. Like the Christian mystics, they may achieve a feeling of pure bliss, extreme happiness, total oneness with nature. The difference is that Jesus and the Holy Spirit are not part of their language.

Does this make the experience invalid? No. Jesus taught that we could all have a closeness to God such as he experienced. He never suggested that only those who professed themselves as Christians could do so; he was a Jew. Typically, the churches chose in general to ignore the New Age or to write it off as Pagan. Little help or understanding has been offered to those of us attempting to remain within the Christian fold. Meditation and personal growth have taken us into a new dimension evidently unacceptable to the priesthood, ministry and hierarchy of the churches. We may therefore need to find our way forward without them. Already there are groups that are on a spiritual path and people have found help through them. I have been particularly helped by CANA (Christians Awakening to a New Awareness) and a Quest Group, which studied the programme under that name. Few of us want to see another institution like the Church. Our habit is to go with a flow that allows the creation and dissolution of temporary structures. What the future holds we do not know, but we are sure that each of us must be responsible for ourselves and not depend on institutions such as the churches have become.

If the organism we call Church is able to recognise the journey being taken by myself and countless others, much of it without its framework, then perhaps there is a future in the Christian fold, but there are many who have been so hurt by the church hierarchy that for them a return to that fold is unthinkable. Do we need a structure for continued development? Although I attend Church fairly regularly, I am not absolutely sure that I 'belong' any more. I am not sure it even matters. What I must not lose sight of is the journey itself. For this I need others to assist in the constant search for understanding, to keep me continually on the quest and not allow atrophy into self-delusion. I believe each one of us has a part to play as midwives to the future. I see a need to live in closer contact with the wholeness of all being. We need to dissolve our edges, open to the requirements of everything around us, work for good, wherever we are called, and seek the infinite wisdom within that can guide us in all we think, do and say so long as we remain connected to the pure source of good.

Update

Journeying towards a Universal Spirituality

Recently, my seventeen-year-old granddaughter asked, 'How can God exist and allow all this suffering in the world?' She then added 'Of course, I don't believe in God.' My husband,

David, and I had recently been to a Modern Church conference entitled 'God, one, three or many.' A lot of what was being said continued the old churchiosity, but there were a number of us voicing our belief in a panentheistic God, that which is in and beyond everything, the force within nature and all creation. I explained to my granddaughter that humanity has free will, and so it is up to each one of us to 'tune in' to this force for the greater good. We are the agents of this God; nothing may be achieved without our will to work towards positive change in the world.

Looking back on the extraordinary experiences and changes in our lives, I feel very fortunate to have lived at this time in history. For David and me, meditation is a strong force in our lives and has seen us through many phases. Now retired, we live next to our village church and have the job of unlocking it each morning. I take the opportunity to go in for a few minutes of silent meditation. Through the way that I believe Jesus showed us in his life, constantly in touch with 'the Father', I make contact with the ultimate force, asking that this day I may act as a human aid in whatever way I am competent. Each day contains some special richness: a chance meeting resulting in deep insight; a wise word coming from somewhere within, dropping into conversation with a troubled soul; discussion groups with all kinds of people not necessarily of Christian persuasion.

We talk of 'Universal Spirituality.' Not wanting to create yet another religion, I see universal spirituality as the binding force that brings us all together with a strong desire for justice, peace, care for others and endeavour to rescue the planet from destruction. Individuals and groups outside any religious persuasion as well as those within specific religious organisations may be party to this in whatever way that allows the freedom to express love and acceptance for all that is.

Kate

Being asked to review one's inner journey can feel a bit like looking at a snakes-and-ladders board – and the dice Life throws you can be very deceptive. The big, fat juicy Six that you thought was bound to land you on an upward soaring ladder in fact lands on a snake, and the miserable little Two that was going nowhere in fact hits a ladder that takes you up through a couple of layers to a new zone of understanding.

My journey started in a down-to-earth Church of England family – Church at Christmas and Easter, and a few extra Sundays in between; followed by a C of E boarding school, chapel twice a day and three times on Sundays. The sparking factor was a mother who increasingly became a freewheeling spirit, and who shared her inner journey with me through my teenage years. So, together we roamed through some more mystic writers than standard Sunday Church fare – William Johnston, Bede Griffiths, Thomas Merton among them – and on towards more esoteric New Age thought like George Trevelyan, Alan Watts, Ram Dass, in particular that certainly loosened things up, and was a wonderful companionship between us.

Then the Six on the dice was marriage, homemaking and two small children. Life became full of practicalities and fun. And God went out the window, except in a taken-for-granted pleasure in the quality of everyday life.

So, to the Two came at around the age of thirty, after a very traumatic miscarriage, in conjunction with the realisation that my marriage was no longer working. There followed several emotionally unhappy years, but then I found myself on a ladder of picking myself up from the pain. The ladder was not the Church, with which I was not in touch, and which seemed to have nothing relevant to offer, but Yoga, which gifted me a miraculous healing of all levels of my being, and also began to make some sense of the pain. It also led to developing in interest in meditation, healing and all things esoteric.

But the spiritual soil my tree is planted in did not want to give up its roots. As my children grew to school age, I found myself wanting them to breathe in all aspects of their heritage, perhaps particularly the Old Testament. So, I sent them to Sunday School. Fine with my daughter, less so with my son, by this time aged four. 'Why should I go to Sunday school if you don't go to Church?' he said. Therefore, I started going to Church again. I discovered a Vicar who talked my language, and preached the Cosmos, and the dance of science and mysticism. We ended up married, and there I am, back in the Church again. Snake or Ladder? A Ladder. I was round a turn of the spiral with a completely different understanding, and now exploring Matthew

□

Fox, Teilhard de Chardin, and astro-physics (as best my limited I.Q. could manage!). The institution of the Church seemed increasingly unimportant, but the precepts of Christianity took on a new meaning and relevance. The Shift, I think, was primarily away from an historically-based Jesus to an opening up of the implications of what some call the Cosmic Christ. It removed for me the limitations and place, and the exclusivity of so much traditional Church teaching. Having dipped a little into other world faiths, especially Buddhism and Hinduism, I have never accepted the Church, or Christianity, as the only path to a relationship with God.

In essence, that is where I still am some twenty years later. The externals of the Game board have taken me through a bereavement, five years alone running a retreat house in a remote corner of Scotland, and now six years married to another dog-collar! A fair mix of the Sixes and Twos. Clearly, I am still connected with the traditional Church through the necessary involvement of being married to it, though most often I feel like a subversive element within. The personal challenge has been to retain a degree of inner integrity in my relationship with the Church while at the same time being true to my own inner voice. And, over the years, I have found myself more and less successful with that – times when I have exploded with frustration, times when I have felt 'That's it,' time to sever the tie but never quite doing it. And the frustration is always with the institution and/or the teachings of the Church, rather than Christianity in so far as

I can interpret it for myself.

Increasingly, I have come to what I call the 'Kitchen sink spirituality,' better known as 'Fetching water, chopping wood.' The externals of life are all as they were before. And yet they're not, because everything is imbued from within with that essence that makes small daily events much larger than the vehicle that carries them. The practicalities of running the retreat house taught me that. And the excitement of the early years of esoteric exploration has melted into a more background but steady pattern of both living the day, and trying to make sense of the messiness and pain of the world and of human beings. I would like to know that All Is Well, rather than All shall be Well. Sometimes I do, sometimes I don't. I believe it, but I don't always know it.

Translated into conventional terms, that has been a journey from depending on the outward rituals and rhythms of the Church (though I still go to Church every Sunday), to looking at the gifts of the day as my teacher and source of inspiration. This is in conjunction with the fundamental precepts of Christianity as I understand it: 'Judge not,' 'Without love all things are worthless,' 'We are called to embody Christ.' I continue to go to Church, partly to support my husband, partly because I believe that in the fragility of humanness both rhythm and discipline are important supports, even when I kick against them. I can still remember the shock of being told twenty years ago, 'You don't go to Church for yourself, you go for all those who do not go.' Not in a holy 'saving sinners' kind of way, but as part of contributing to what some call 'the Prayer of the whole Church.' That phrase still has an exclusivity about it for me, so I prefer to think of it as each person's contribution to turning the Prayer Wheel of the World. That is essentially a selfless act, but of course in turn it nourishes me, too.

Living where I do, i.e., in a relatively conservative backwater, there is not a great deal in the overt life of the Church to nourish my inner world. Snake or Ladder? Again, I have come to think Ladder, because it has pushed me to look within, to work things out for myself, to learn from direct experience, to find my own truth, with the help of course of many Wise Beings who have crossed my path, either directly or through books. There is always a danger here of arrogance, leaving the well-trodden path to go up one's own cul-de-sac. But maybe that too just gets composted in. Experience is my teacher, and I need to remind myself that often the most difficult people, the most difficult situations, are the things I most need to grow and to learn. It may not be the obvious inspiration of a deep meditation retreat or an uplifting talk, but it can be the most effective chisel to chip away at the 'self-encapsulated ego,' especially if I am aware enough to cooperate with the process.

More obviously, I draw nourishment from the natural world around me. Living in the dramatic and awe-inspiring scenery of N.W. Scotland, it is not hard to feel in touch with That in which I live and move and have my being, as the seasons of light and dark, and the forceful weather patterns come and go. And from meditation, too, whether it be the more formal 'sitting' or a looser kind of watching the sea and cloudscapes. Much of what I have learned at this level has come from Eastern teachings rather than Christian sources, but I think mainly because these were more accessible to me. In essence, I do not think there is much difference in the awareness both would lead us to, only perhaps in the detail of the scenery through which we travel on the way.

That of course might well be questioned by much of traditional Christianity, which remains wary of anything not coming directly from the Church. For myself, I have come to trust the feel of direct experience over the voice of the expert whose path is different from mine, despite the obvious damage here of self-delusion. I recognise that most of the great Christian mystics of the past, Merton and Teilard de Chardin among them, remained anchored within the Church, and perhaps that is another reason I choose not to leave it entirely, despite so much dogma I cannot subscribe to. This requires me to stay very quiet in most Christian company, for fear of further burnings-at-the-stake, as it were.

So, the vision that moves me forward is of contributing even a small part of a monkey to the Hundredth Monkey Syndrome that will enable the human race to take its next leap in the evolution of consciousness. (This refers to Lyall Watson's research that once a critical number of monkeys was reached, i.e., the hundredth monkey, a behaviour previously learned by conventional means of observation and repetition instantly spread across the water to other monkeys by a sort of group consciousness.) Gerard Hughes asks, 'When will the children-of-God grow up to be the adults-of-God?' I would like to think that will happen when we cling less fearfully to our own particular dogma, when we see our truth as a facet of Truth rather than The Truth. And when we stop looking exclusively to an external saviour, anchored in time and history, to save us from ourselves. Rather perhaps we need to start taking a personal responsibility for so much of what the New Testament guides us towards. We are called to be Christ in the World, which merely requires the removal of all our ego, all our self-interest...

And so back to the kitchen sink, which I have found is the best classroom for learning such things. Inspired teachers, whether in the flesh or in books, continue to re-motivate me on the journey of living, but at the end of the day the homework is mine, and I have a strong sense that it is more who we are than what we say that contributes to humanity's development. These are the shortcuts to beingness. So, I continue to travel with the Church, though the Institution frequently irritates me beyond belief. This is partly because I think that the human race is not yet mature enough to live without institutions, and that I feel that at least some of us need to work for change from within rather than abandon ship altogether.

I also continue to travel with Christianity because, despite all I have learnt from the East and from more esoteric ways of thought, it still provides me with the most comprehensive and inclusive philosophy that embraces light and dark, materiality and spirituality, joy and sorrow, and gives meaning through the transforming power of love to the anguish and the pain we see all around us. Perhaps one day I will wake up embedded in the consciousness of non-duality that I know to be there but keep slipping out of. Perhaps that is the end of the journey. Perhaps that is the final ladder to the top of the board.

Update

Becoming who I really am

Since moving from Scotland to Cornwall eight-and-a-half years ago, I have learnt and experienced some more about non-dual consciousness. Amongst these lessons is that it is not just one simple last ladder up to attain it, but more of a stop/start slowly incremental journey to work towards it amidst the circumstances of our dualistic everyday world which, it seems, constantly try to tug us back into the old level of awareness. The challenge is to keep working at opening into this new way of being while remaining within the dualistic mindset so firmly embedded in our culture. That is certainly an inner-muscle-strengthening exercise for which I find a number of reference point questions helpful, if I can pause long enough to ask myself one or two of them.

-Am I 'responding' or 'reacting?' (Cynthia Bourgeault would say, 'Am I in the 'Brace' position?')!

-Am I seeing this situation from a 'both/and,' or an 'either/or' mindset?

-Am I excluding, or am I transcending and including?

-Does what I say or do empower, or disempower, the other person?

These are practical exercises, not in themselves non-dualistic, but helping me to move in that direction.

Not long after moving to Cornwall, I had a brief but powerful experience, the meaning of which I have continued to ponder ever since. I am not given to 'seeing' spirits, or those I have loved who have died. But I was suddenly aware in the middle of one night of my deceased husband, Jack, standing by my bedside. He simply said to me 'You have come to Cornwall to become who you really are.' And then he vanished again.

I could come up with a number of versions of 'who I really am,' but my two strongest images are:

First, the image of an acorn that spends much of its Acorn-life rolling around on the ground being an acorn, until one day it looks up from under a mighty, mature oak tree and realises 'Oh my goodness, THAT's what I could become.'

And second, the image of a teaspoon of mustard in a vinaigrette dressing, whose presence stops the oil and vinegar from separating after they have been shaken together.

Both these images need some unpacking.

I equate the Acorn with my personality, which has spent much of its life giving itself a good polish and brush up. Nothing wrong with that, except that at some point the Acorn has to take the risk of cracking open its shell (usually not an entirely pain-free experience) in order to begin to realise its potential as an Oak tree

– which is what 'I really am.' This appears to be my inner work now.

And being the 'mustard' in the Vinaigrette is part of that for me, the Oil and the Vinegar representing Spirit and Matter, which so often get dualistically separated in our thinking and in our living. As I attempt to grow towards my fully realised oak tree, I need to integrate them, both within myself and in the world in which I live, until I am living in a stable condition of knowing them as one infused substance.

Meanwhile, still married to my much beloved Dog collar, I try to weave all this in and out of the rhythms of the Christian year, and if not frequently in church, where I find much of the liturgy pulling me backwards into the old ways of being, then at least mindful of the Seasons, and the archetypes of the great Christian festivals and what they represent in my own inner journey of transformation.

I have found the writings of Cynthia Bourgeault and Richard Rohr particularly helpful as contemporary writers finding a language for our times. And, of course, the mystic writers from all strands of Christianity from the desert fathers and mothers onwards have played their part in bringing us to this point in evolution.

The journey to the top of the Board continues – definitely still a game in progress, but perhaps up a ladder or two from a decade ago, and now with a slightly wider horizon.

Voices of Acceptance

'All healthy religion shows you what to do with your pain. Great religion shows you what to do with the absurd, the tragic, the nonsensical, the unjust. If we do not transform this pain, we will most assuredly transmit it to others...'[1]

Richard Rohr

Sometimes new insights are hard won and come as a result of times that can seem dark, or described as a breakdown, while old forms disintegrate before there is a breakthrough to a new way of perceiving reality and a new sense of self. The next couple of biographies detail some of this pathway, and the difficult terrain it has entailed.

Mary Jo

I was born in September, 1939 into a very traditional Roman Catholic family going right back to times of persecution when some of my ancestors died for the Faith. This was the heritage passed onto us. I had five brothers and always felt a bit of a misfit and of little worth. Maybe that had some bearing on my decision to enter the convent at 17 years of age. I wanted my life to be worthwhile and, in my upbringing, the best thing you could do was to give it to God in Religious life.

Having been at boarding school at the convent, it seemed the natural place to enter. As a child I had dyslexia, not diagnosed in those days, so I was considered stupid. So, when I entered, I was labelled 'practical,' needing no training. In my innocence and naivety, I presumed I should do whatever the superior said. After all, I had taken a vow of Obedience, besides I did not know what else I could do. I thought this would enable me to develop a good relationship with God. In total dedication, I followed the rules and directions to the letter, and lived a very dedicated and rigid life. I became God's best conformist.

By the age of 43, I reached total breakdown, I was totally exhausted and had nothing left to give. I reached a moment of looking at the moon shining on railway lines and seeing it as a positive choice to end it now so that someone else could do my job properly. If I had nothing to give, then my life was worth nothing. At this point, Providence stepped in: I bumped into a therapist, not knowing either that she was one or what therapy was!

Working with her, I gradually found a new world opening up. With her encouragement and support, I went for an interview at a Catholic college to do a Postgraduate Diploma. I did not even have A levels and knew I could not possibly do it. To my astonishment, they accepted me. I was now in secular dress, feeling very vulnerable and convinced once they discovered how bad I was I would be asked to leave, then what? For the first time, questions were not only acceptable but encouraged. My Catholic faith was being explored in the context of its history and development. I remember writing my first essay and gave it in with such trepidation. After a week the tutor summoned me to her office and handed it back. I turned it over. There was nothing at the end, so I knew it was not good enough. She smiled and said, 'There is a green piece of paper inside'. I looked, and it said A. I handed it back and said "You've given me the wrong one." She said, 'No I have not, this is your mark.' I was stunned and from then on could enjoy the course.

My appetite had been whetted and I wanted more. Most sisters had had a three-year degree course and a one-year teacher's training so I thought I could ask for more. I applied to Heythrop in London, which was a Jesuit College and considered Academic. I did not think I would get in, but I did. I was told to find a Spiritual Director, which I was happy to do. I loved it all, and soon realised I could not possibly go back to the Convent. The Spiritual Director was in agreement but was concerned as to how I would earn a living, as indeed I was – well more than concerned, terrified. I just wanted to be ordinary, yet I knew little of that life. Work, clothes, money, food would all be a challenge.

I imagined I could do Parish work but was quickly told that no one would employ me with my background, and anyway they would not pay me a living wage. There were some very dark times. I remember standing in Battersea Rise, thinking, *Who is going to buy my toothbrush? Mary Jo, no one is going to buy your toothbrush.* I cleaned and ironed for about five years. That did teach me about ordinary life, but I feared that after all the effort to leave this would be all I would ever be doing. In hindsight, when my work opened up I needed to have been through such an experience so as to understand the kind of life my clients were coping with.

I belonged to a very forward-looking community with a priest at its head. We used to go to a cellar-like room underneath the Leister Square Church where the liturgies were created by the community, but still the priest had the final say. It did open up the possibility of creative liturgies. Soon after I moved on, I remember the first time I decided that going to Mass was too painful and was not feeding my soul. I went for a walk in Cannizaro Park, experienced the birds as my choir, the trees as my cathedral, the plants and flowers as my reading and source of reflection. The natural world has continued to feed my soul ever since. One weekend, when I was utterly exhausted, I looked up a Convent by the sea, thinking how nourishing it would be to walk in the sun by the sea. I thought they might be able to offer me an inexpensive break.

I arrived and it poured with rain unremittingly, no nice walks by the sea on the sand. One of the sisters showed me the library full of interesting books, but what caught my eye was a video, *The Hidden Heart of the Cosmos* with Brian Swimme. Eventually I found someone to show me how to play the video. I was captivated and inspired by his spiritual approach, the depth

□

and width of it touched my Soul. here was a Spiritual path I could follow of Cosmic dimensions. I was both deeply moved and expanded by it. I saved the small amount of money I had and purchased the twelve videos *The Canticle of the Cosmos*.

By now my work had taken a leap forward. I had set up 'Coping with change,' which evolved out my initial inability to deal with change and I began to wonder if I was the only one who found it difficult. I was working with both individuals and groups, which I loved. I longed to share these videos and so The Cosmic group was born. We still meet about every six weeks to listen, share, explore and deepen our understanding of it all. Brian Swimme is a Mathematical Cosmologist, and we grapple with the material, but he is an American and wonderful communicator who both challenges, stimulates and inspires us. Together we travel this broad and deep path, and out of it grew the desire to hold a Cosmic Holy week. So, each year a group of us go somewhere beautiful to explore the depth and meaning of these days and create our own relevant Cosmic Liturgies and spiritual expressions. It is a deeply collaborative experience and continues to this day. I see these days as the heart of the liturgical year and want to take time out to understand and celebrate them. Every year is different because we are different, and the world has changed. Though it can be quite challenging to bring all the strands of inspiration together, we both struggle with it and love it, and it expands our souls.

I still needed to solve my desire for a more regular

Eucharist. I tried many churches and groups, yet none felt very nourishing, nor did I feel spiritually at home. After some time, I decided I would start a small group who would meet to celebrate the Solstice and Equinox to honour the turning points of the year. They are held in my flat using the format of a Eucharist and with the consecration prayer of Teilhard de Chardin's Mass on the world, developed when he was in France in the trenches. We have no priest and those present bring all kinds of contributions. We believe that it is the community who make Christ present in the bread and wine.

I still have a desire for a more frequent celebration of the Eucharist, so each Sunday I celebrate it in my flat by myself yet inviting the whole Universe to be present. I find this answers my need well enough for now, though I believe nothing is forever. I still have a thirst for ongoing learning, development and new experiences. Every morning I go to a coffee shop for an hour to read and reflect on a Spiritual book. I both work and live on my own, so I like to start the day connecting with the outside world. I value both formal and informal meditation. The natural world continues to feed my Soul as I immerse myself in the essence of its beauty. Having no garden, I am a frequent visitor to Kew Gardens or anywhere I can find quiet in the natural world.

Yet I live in Clapham Junction, the hub of the train Universe and a real union of the opposites. I respect all faiths and none, and have a passion for the Spiritual dimension of everything and everyone. If something feeds my Soul, I will hope to experience it and if it does not I will let it go. My life is full of gratitude for the small things and remains open to wonder, awe and amazement. I also endeavour to embrace and learn from the shadow side. I very much like the interpretation of the yin and yang where the white is 'crisis' and the black is 'opportunity.' This seems so relevant to where we are now as we struggle to make sense of the global pandemic. By holding the opposites, I desire to be open to the new thing that comes out of holding this tension.

So, I have in some senses travelled full circle in my desire to live a full and meaningful life, not by a route I could have planned myself, but am truly grateful for all the help, guidance and inspiration I have received on the way. I would now describe myself as a Spiritual Seeker open to continually expanding my horizons with fellow travellers and desiring to send the energy of loving kindness and compassion to our precious and beautiful planet and all life on it.

Janet

My own journey has been challenging and taken me through many dark places. I am not sure I would have come through without the gift of a deep sense of the spiritual dimension from quite early in my life. I was brought up with virtually no teaching about spirituality, my father being a professed atheist and my mother a nominal Presbyterian. We did have to attend Matins on Christmas Day and Easter Day at the local parish church for social reasons before we were allowed to open presents, and how long and tedious those services felt! Despite this, as a teenager, I found myself reading books on mysticism and concentration camps picked up from jumble sales, reading them under the bedclothes in case anyone saw me. Most especially I didn't want to be seen reading anything on mysticism as my family would have regarded that as very odd indeed.

At university, I was deeply struck by two sayings in a couple of books, which have stayed with me ever since: 'Keep thy mind in hell and despair not', and 'All shall be well, and all manner of things shall be well' (the first from *The Undistorted Image* by Sofrony about Staretz Silouan, a hermit on Mount Athos,[2] the second from *Revelations of Divine Love* by Julian of Norwich, an anchoress).[3] I also had a keen sense of being part of the whole of humanity and therefore responsible as much as anyone else for all the disasters in the world, but I did not understand the notion of non-duality (which is about transcending opposites), and therefore identified too much at the personal level. It was a kind of negative inflation that led to all sorts of difficulties until I learned a vital secret of the spiritual life: of being a true witness to what is, however horrendous or joyful, but of not identifying with any of it.

In 1967, I spent a summer vacation in Palestine/Israel just after the six-day war and this was a watershed moment. The pain and suffering of many there and the inhumanity of others turned my whole world upside down and inside out. I was in a bad state when I returned to university, but the chaplain was sensitive and, rather than referring me to the student counselling service, suggested I spoke with the wise and deeply spiritual head of an enclosed contemplative community (Anglican Carmelites). I kept returning there without knowing why and it was some years before I recognised consciously that their contemplative life offered a framework both wide enough and deep enough to contain that experience. So, I was introduced very early in my adult life to the mystical tradition of Christianity and to the necessity of a daily spiritual practice.

Experiencing parochial life of the Church of England was a real shock after university. I just couldn't resonate with all the dogma, doctrine and theology that appeared to assume that one way was right and another wrong, nor with the wordiness and lack of silence in the liturgy. The mystical way I'd been introduced to in the contemplative religious community seemed to be about the idea of our one-ness with all through letting go, self-emptying (kenosis), and silence. I was being increasingly drawn to this more unitive consciousness (which some call non-dual spirituality), which embraces the paradox of being uniquely the person I am whilst simultaneously being one with all. I'm a drop in the ocean and the ocean is in the drop.

My first conscious awareness of one-ness was on Iona when I was about 27. I had climbed Duni, the highest point, and was awe-struck by the magnificence of the panorama set before me: the scattered range of islands emerging from the turquoise and ultramarine sea. I felt very small compared with the magnitude of the beauty I was witnessing and then it was as though I was drawn up into it and there was no longer any separation. In that moment, this glorious aspect of the natural world and I were one, a moment beyond all duality, which I've never forgotten. I've occasionally known this sense of oneness when in love, experiencing no separation between me and my beloved and, simultaneously, feeling at one with all peoples and the whole cosmos. This has mirrored my understanding of the relationship with the divine, as lover and beloved.

In 1988 I had a 'breakdown,' which was another watershed moment in my spiritual awakening. (I use inverted commas as it was really a 'breakthrough.') I was to find God in the depths rather than in the heights and there was a coming together of my psychological and spiritual searching, which I'd kept very separate until then. I came to realise they had been interweaving, creating a tapestry of what my life is about. I learned, most importantly, that I was being asked to welcome and embrace all experiences that come my way as fully as I am able, whether pleasant or unpleasant, because in as far as I was involved in the work of healing or transforming them at the personal level, I was contributing to the healing of that aspect of the human condition. 'You can only redeem that which is lived' (ancient proverb), and I also became increasingly aware in my work as a psychotherapist that those with some of the most awful stories were being entrusted with a lot to redeem.

Two years after my breakdown, I was giving a talk at the

University of Life in London entitled *Out of my Love for You I will Give You Back to Yourself*. I could not have given this particular talk without the experience of that breakdown, and in the question time a man in his mid-fifties got up, said he was Jewish, and having felt he could do nothing other than hate all Nazis, especially Nazi war criminals, had found himself moved for this man I'd been describing. I'd given an example of my title with recounting the work of a journalist, Gitta Sereny (from her book *Into That Darkness*), of her interviews with Franz Stangl in prison, the commandant of the Treblinka concentration camp.[4] He was an Austrian policeman with a young family, offered a job which got him on the first rung of the SS ladder, which if he'd refused, meant he would not get a job at all. But it was a ladder increasingly hard to get off without putting at risk his own life and that of his family. That night I wept, that this man at the talk, given some understanding behind the story of Franz Stangl, had found within himself compassion for him. I knew for the first time then that my breakdown had not been the curse I'd felt it to be but a real blessing.

Another period of my life stands out as a time of deep spiritual awakening when I lived on the Isle of Iona for two years, 1996-1998. I went when I was very broken, having lost all trust in both myself and others, but following a deep intuition to go against the advice of almost everyone I knew because of the state I was in. For the first time in my adult life, I was without my roles as mother and professional and I had not realised the extent to which my sense of who I was had become utterly dependent on those. It was like dropping into a horrendous void and having no identity☐ a stripping away, a very necessary stripping away. This time was a period of deep healing for me, and I quote:

> I am not a mechanism, an assembly of various sections.
> And it is not because the mechanism is working wrongly that I am ill. I am ill because of wounds to the soul, to the deep emotional self, and wounds to the soul take a long, long time. Only time can help, and patience, and a certain difficult repentance, long difficult repentance, realisation of life's mistake, and the freeing oneself from the endless repetition of the mistake which mankind at large has chosen to sanctify.[5] (D.H. Lawrence)

Time is not usually allowed for such healing in our society where there is such emphasis on getting back to how we were before, to a time when our functioning was seemingly satisfactory enough. Yet the journey of the soul will have its way to restore us to our true self; and the broken relationship, the loss of a dear one, work problems, injury or illness, etc. become its window of opportunity. I was fortunate to have time, time I needed, and time some deep knowing part of myself required me to take.

I said I had come to experience a more contemplative way of being, but what did that mean? The island taught me. As I wandered, sat, watched, and waited, the island began to reveal more of her secrets to me☐ mirroring how it is in the spiritual life. The slowing down to have time for each moment brought a new level of receptivity in me and, as a way of putting it (for words are so clumsy), an increasing sense of living from the dimension of soul rather than from the dimension of personality, to coin Andrew Harvey's phrase. It felt like a shift from the drivenness of my ego to the spaciousness of spirit, and this was, and is, the most precious gift imaginable. I grieve each time I lose connection to it.

Also, the way I felt, the island received and listened to me is encapsulated in a saying by Lao-Tsze, (with me replacing 'he' and 'his' with 'she' and 'hers'):

> 'It is as though she listened
> And such listening as hers
> enfolds us in a silence
> In which at last
> we begin to hear
> What we are meant to be.'[6]

Of course, I was later to realise that this was the quality of listening I was accessing within my own being – that inner knowing – which at that point I was projecting onto the island, just as clients project upon counsellors what eventually they discover is within themselves. When ownership happens, then access to it is no longer dependent on actual connection with us and they can leave more whole. So, it was with my relationship with Iona.

Mary Oliver puts it so well in her amazing poem *The Journey.*

At this stage, I became aware of a shift going on within. The inner pilgrimage initially had thrown me into a terrible void, and at first I'd had to deal with lots of unresolved emotional pain and psychological issues. And I nearly gave up at that stage. I had to wake up to the degree of bondage to the past and befriend and integrate that as all part of what it means to be human, warts and all – to honour this as my particular version of the human story just as, hopefully, I would honour another's. I began to recognise the nature of the process happening to me on the island step by step: that, by letting go of the conditioning factors that told me how I ought to be and my ego's need to control, I was increasingly free to be myself. 'Being nothing... but the rich lens of attention' is a very different kind of void to that I experienced at the beginning of my time on Iona. I sincerely believe, until we have woken up to that voice within and have access to our inner knowing, it is unlikely we can embrace a more non-dual consciousness or even explore a more universal spirituality. Yet how vital a task that is!

I'd become disillusioned with the way the Christian tradition was presenting itself, as it was so dualistic. I'd seriously considered whether I could go on calling myself Christian, as most of what was going on in church, and being taught there, found no resonance within me. But then, about ten years ago, I came across *The Wisdom Jesus* by Cynthia Bourgeault, which was transformative. This book described what I knew deep within me but didn't know I knew. There was a big 'yes' to this understanding of what Christianity is all about and I'd met aspects of it within the mystical traditions of some contemplative communities I'd known since student days. I was fortunate enough to get a place on her first Wisdom School retreat on Holy Island (off Arran) and what a hugely enlightening experience that was. It confirmed what I knew in the depths of my being, that Jesus was showing us the way of transformation to the sense of oneness (or unitive consciousness). She says to reach this point, we need to spend more time in contemplative silence:

'Every spiritual tradition that holds a vision of human transformation at its heart claims that a practice of intentional silence is a non-negotiable... essential to spiritual awakening.'[7]

We are living in a world dominated, certainly in the West, by self-interest, greed, and fear, and with ways of thinking and being that foster polarisation and conflict. Increasingly 'my' or 'our' safety, security and standard of living are threatened by the different other. So it's my (or our) self-interest as opposed to yours – me or you, rather than me and you as part of the one whole body of humanity with concern for the wellbeing of all. Surely our relationship to the earth and to one another has to change radically for the future life of our and other species on this beautiful planet earth. It won't come about by counteraction as that merely fuels the polarising or dualistic way of being. There needs to be a collective shift in consciousness from being trapped in the heavy energies of living from a separative perspective alone, to that life-giving and lighter energy of cooperation with the unseen realms, those spiritual dimensions.

The exploration of a more universal spirituality seems vital to me if we are to meet the challenges of the day from a creative and unifying place, rather than a destructive and divisive one. But how to access that? What encourages me is the real hunger I see in many people for an authentic and living spirituality emerging anew from its roots in the mystical heart of all the faith traditions, but reawakened and revitalised to be accessible and relevant in this day and age. As the mystic Meister Eckhart said:

'The outer work can never be small if the inner work is great. And the outer work can never be great if the inner work is small.'[8]

Voices of Discovery

These writers, whilst alluding to many of the themes in other biographies, illustrate something of the struggle or journey that had to be taken for transformation and authenticity to emerge. The words of the Catholic poet Gerard Manley Hopkins are just below. When talking of such deep and difficult journeys, he exhorts those who have not found themselves in such terrain not to 'hold them cheap.'

> O the mind, mind has mountains: cliffs of fall
> Frightful, sheer, no-man-fathomed. Hold them cheap
> May who ne'er hung there.[1]

Judy

Where do we come from; what are we; where are we going? (The title of a painting by Gauguin)

Since I was a child, I have been conscious of a strong inner feeling that there existed a benevolent creative force behind the universe. This conviction originated, I think, in a term spent at a Roman Catholic convent when I was seven. Luckily, because I was not a Catholic, no one tried to catechise me; I was just given an attractive little booklet saying that Jesus cared for me, and I was allowed to absorb the atmosphere of the chapel, which I found deeply satisfying. There was something there that I wanted, and this stayed with me all through the rest of my school career, when prayers and hymns at assemblies failed to make any impression. In fact, they were all about social control and nothing to do with true holiness or a sense of the sacred.

The experience at the convent coincided with a short period when my family lived in the Kentish countryside in what my mother, a Londoner, thought of as a grotty cottage, miles from anywhere. But for me, the whole of that small world within walking distance of home was deeply numinous. The orchard at the back of the house was full of wild daffodils in the spring and the banks were thick with primroses. The wood at the bottom of the steep lane passing our cottage was dominated by a huge beech tree on a mound – so obviously a sacred place, though I could not have put this thought into words at that age. This time, which looking back feels almost like a period outside time, before the stresses of the world impinged, was the foundation of a sense of wonder that has stayed with me all my life and has sustained me in difficult times.

I was a shy and dreamy child, an observer rather than a participant in life, always trying to figure out what life was all about and why other people acted as they did. Books provided some of the answers, but I was never sure where I fitted into things or what my role should be.

At the age of seventeen, a churchgoing friend introduced me to a gentle Anglican priest named Berners-Wilson (his daughter, Angela, was the first woman to be ordained in the Church of England). Together, my friend and I walked four or five miles on quiet roads through the attractive Kentish countryside on Sunday mornings to attend communion in his church at Frant, and hear him preach about that 'unseen hidden world which is all about us.' Looking back, I can see that he would have fitted very comfortably into the tradition later labelled 'Creation Spirituality,' a tradition that emphasised the blessings of life rather than dwelling on our sinfulness.

Somehow, through young adulthood and middle age, I managed to avoid contact with anyone who tried to put constraints on the development of my faith. Encountering some inspiring teachers from different Christian traditions on the way, I eventually discovered the Ignatian tradition. Again, I was lucky with my mentors, enlightened nuns and Jesuits who believed strongly that God meets each person where they are and that this crucial relationship should be nurtured, but not impeded by what Gerard Hughes called 'the tyranny of the oughteries.'

It was only when I came across the Alpha course in my local church ('three reasons to prove that God exists: one, two, three!') that I realised with intense shock how unorthodox my belief system appeared to be. This led to several years of painful struggle in which I felt quite unable to fit into the framework of conventional Christianity. Who was Jesus, this person who has felt like a friend and companion on the Way? Is he merely an archetype constellated by my own unconscious psyche, as some Jungian psychologists suggest? Why the emphasis on suffering instead of blessing, on sin rather than redemption, crucifixion rather than resurrection? What do all these words that theologians use mean anyway, and are they at all relevant to everyday life?

The struggle to find a place for my own spirituality within a church community continues, but in the process, the members of the congregation I worship with have become very dear to me and those I know well have been accepting of my need to ask searching questions. A small group meets midweek using the Iona *Wee Worship Book*. The beautifully phrased Celtic prayers in this book seem so much more relevant to everyday life than those in the Sunday service. This session, and the opportunity it offers to share our current concerns, have become very important for me. Also, I feel strongly that a welcoming village church still has a part to play at the centre of a community, offering support in celebrating happy events such as marriage and baptism and solace in times of grief and loss, when many people who are not regular churchgoers come together for a funeral.

My bookshelves groan with books on all kinds of spirituality: Christian, Buddhist, Jewish, Sufi, shamanistic. Bede Griffiths, Andrew Harvey, Anthony de Mello, Jack Kornfield are some of the authors who have helped me in the past, and more recently Richard Rohr and Cynthia Bourgeault have brought important new insights and 'aha' moments with their fairly radical rethink of theology. A whole shelf is devoted to near-death experiences as the inner searching of my more mature days was triggered by the very vivid experience of the presence of a close friend who had recently died. There are books on reincarnation too, including the *Tibetan Book of Living and Dying*, which, for me, makes a lot of sense.

In the past I have found the Cygnus booklist very useful in adding to this collection, although recently I seem to have gone beyond the need to read about other people's experience (with the exception of this wonderful account of the experiences of CANA friends), and that I need to look inside myself to find answers. Perhaps this change of orientation is one of the fruits of old age, when one attempts to draw together the lessons of life; re-reading James Fowlers' *Stages of Faith* is helping to make sense of this process.

Although I have been a student of the work of Carl Jung and other psychologists over the last thirty years, I don't see how psychology alone can provide all the answers. Jung himself wrote extensively about his spiritual journey, which included a vivid near-death experience and which, in his strange and beautiful Red Book, took him to some unusual places. His response to John Freeman's question about belief in God ('I don't need to believe, I know') was later expanded on in another interview in which he said: 'I could not say I believe. I know! I have had the experience of being gripped by something that is stronger than myself, something that people call God.'[2] But, and this is a big but, he went on to explain that this was not necessarily what practising Christians mean when they talk about believing in God. (See the website of The Uncertaintist April 23, 2012.)

Words are not always adequate to describe one's inner process and I turn more and more to music and art, which convey a meaning beyond words. However, E. E. Cummings' poem does a good job of conveying what I feel (on a good day!): 'I thank you God for most this amazing day; for the leaping greenly spirits of the trees and the blue true dream of sky and for everything that is natural, that is infinite, that is yes.'[3]

Saying yes to life, whatever it brings, is so important.

Update

I lost my husband soon after writing this piece for CANA, so came to rely for friendship, interest, and solace on groups of people outside the family, my children having grown up and flown the nest. I have helped to set up and facilitate small groups under the auspices of the Cambridge Jungian Circle and have formed close friendships with shared interests within this context. However, I still retain the slightly uncomfortable feeling of not quite fitting with any of the groups I belong to, including in this the village church I attend. My churchgoing friends are puzzled that I cannot just 'accept the whole package,' while my Jungian friends are puzzled as to why I hang on in with the church, feeling that the Christian 'myth' is no longer relevant. This feeling of being on the edge is shared by many members of CANA and it has been wonderful to be part of the Core Group where each member's spiritual path can be shared, accepted and enabled in a non-judgemental way. I think that Richard Rohr's definition of a mystic: 'one who has moved from mere belief or belonging systems to actual inner experience of God' would apply to many members of CANA, though some of them would leave God out of this.[4]

I enjoy accompanying others as they explore their spiritual paths. Sometimes this involves just listening, sometimes a conversation about the deeper aspects of life. The other day someone asked me what gave me pleasure. The answer is 'so many things:' family, friends, films, books, paintings, colour, 'aha' moments of understanding, but also the village church that has provided a stable framework for my spirituality over the last thirty years, despite my difficulties with theology. It would be hard to find other places where one can express so fully the gratitude just for being alive within God's glorious creation, and the sadness that we, as humans, do so many things to sully it. Psychology, for me, does not provide a satisfactory container for these feelings, or a comprehensive explanation of the spiritual impulse. A village church is still, in many ways, at the centre of a community, where people can choose to come and celebrate the milestones of life.

As quoted above, E.E. Cummings' poem *I thank you God for most this amazing day* expresses this feeling for me. I learned from a self-help book that practically saved my life during an episode of depression when I was young that saying an emphatic 'yes' to life is the most important thing, whatever it brings. It is impossible to be grateful and depressed at the same time! I have also learnt since, that it is what one puts into the groups like CANA, my local church and the various discussion groups in which I participate that matters, not what one expects to get out of them. I am responsible for my life; no one else is.

Sue

I am so glad to be where I am today. My life has many unknowns and uncertainties, but I would not go back. I want to choose the road less travelled, an open way with much unexplored territory.

Looking back ten years, I see someone who thought that they knew what life was about. Moreover, I thought I knew what God was all about. I am probably being too hard on myself to say that I was trapped in an ecclesiological system but nonetheless the question that shaped my thinking was more around the 'how' of communicating and living the gospel than the 'who' and 'what' of God.

From that ten-year perspective, I would be astounded to see myself today rarely attending a church service on a Sunday. Since childhood and particularly in adolescence, 'going to church' was always a pleasure, not a duty. Regular times of quiet for prayer, bible reflection and journal writing were the lifelines of my adult life. So, what is so different today?

A large part of the difference is doubtless related to the creativity of the second half of life. As I often say to friends reaching the fiftieth watershed, 'Nothing to prove, nothing to lose!' My mid–life crisis (opportunity) took off around my mid-forties. A phase of self-discovery and exploration was launched and enhanced by choosing to do some further study in the form of a Diploma in Pastoral Counselling and an MTh in Applied Theology. The former opened up life-changing reflection on my own story, especially the effects of my mother's death when I was five years old. I reconnected with my humanity as distinct from defining myself from my God. I saw that God makes us primarily 'human,' not 'Christian.' At that stage my experience of my humanity included the death of my father and a significant new friendship. Teilhard de Chardin's insight is instructive: '...the overflowing tenderness of those special preferential loves which you implant in our lives as the most powerful created agent of our inward growth.'[5]

From my MTh studies I lit upon Iranaeus' observation in the sixth century that, 'the glory of God is the human person fully alive.'[6] This felt electrifying in its liberating implications. This focus on my and everyone's sacred human origin was in no way to negate the very real experience of the heart, which I had known as my Christian 'conversion.' It simply put it in another perspective, one which is proving to be deliciously more open-ended, if not loose-ended.

The shift to a more open arena was also triggered by an ecclesiastical shock. During a two-year period as a full time, paid, lay pastoral coordinator in a team of four churches, I found myself excluded from the weekly staff meetings. This was my first experience of clericalism. Shocks, while painful, can be good for the soul. For me this was the equivalent of a seismic shift. Ten years later, part of its fruit is an evolving network of conversations around the country of those not afraid to be called 'boat-rockers.' Within that I have my personal conviction that ordination threatens the flourishing of both clergy and laity.

However, I remain passionate about the worth of every one of the people of God. My shock was all the greater because for so long my being part of the body of Christ had been such a rich experience. This remains a reality today but not one expressed in Sunday liturgies. In my determination to 'live my adventure,' a phrase I prefer to 'vocation,' I have travelled a path littered with some amazing people, not all of whom would see themselves as Christian. In one sense this no longer matters. They are people from God. I relish my interaction with them. They no longer need to fit my system. I am not afraid of difference.

Indeed, one of my goals for the coming year is to track down a small number of people of other faiths, or no faith at all, who would be interested in a regular conversation. A look through my current pile of books reveals a further exploration of difference and dialogue. N. T. Wright and Marcus Borg's searching *The Meaning of Jesus* in such a generous spirit; Karen Armstrong's fascinating historical analysis of fundamentalism in *The Battle for God*; *Friends on the Way: A life enriched by engagement with people of many faiths* by Maureen Henderson, and the writings of Emily

Carr, the Canadian artist whose experience of First Nation spirituality is awesome.

The conviction of the creativity of difference has been one of the fruits of my belonging to an open-ended therapy group for the past five years. Here I was privileged to witness the sacredness of our human interaction, the human dynamic that images the wonder of God. Here I saw hope for the world. Would that our churches held such circles of difference!

I recall the evening I attended an Iona liturgy in the ancient chapel in Bradwell. It should have been beautiful but I experienced it as stultifying. It was only as I came out of the building and beheld the sky that I worshipped. At that moment I breathed deep. Energy was outside.

Energy has become a familiar word as I have listened to friends in CANA. Facilitating – a group who are considering creating a therapeutic centre, I find myself using the language of going with the energy of God rather than praying for something to happen. I also recognise that some of what gave me energy ten years ago remains true today. My recent consultancy publicity leaflet describes me as aiming towards 'The hearty singing out by ordinary people of what too often lies withering in their hearts.' I came across that sentence in a novel by Dorothy Canfield. It moved me then and it does so now.

There are differing nuances but continuing themes in my life. God is in me and I in God – we have journeyed together for a long time. I am so grateful for the people who continue to challenge me and check me and assure me that it is good to be me. I continue to meet with my spiritual director who has accompanied my journey for over ten years. It was she who asked me what would it mean to take a risk in my relating to God. Listening to the self within, I seek to continue to risk.

I began by saying I am grateful to be where I am today. In practical terms, that means living in a beautiful house that is not mine and being partially dependant for my income on the gifts of Christian friends who believe in the journey I have chosen, not knowing what kind of home will be mine in a year's time. That too is energising.

> *O God*
> *Who am I now?*
> *Once I was secure*
> *In familiar territory*
> *In my sense of belonging*
> *Unquestioning of the names of my culture*
> *The assumptions built into my language*
> *The values shared by my society*
> *But now you have called me out away from home...*[7]

Kate Compston, England, 1990 From *Bread of Tomorrow: Prayers for the Church Year*

Update

I've just been looking at what I wrote previously. In the process I've read what I'd written in my journal as I celebrated my

70th birthday. 'No: 'No plans – bliss. The joy of the empty space!'

Yet my 'spirituality' is a continuum. If I have a conscious contribution, in whatever time I have left, it is to continue to bring to voice those who feel their voice is irrelevant – give significance to each voice. 'I' cannot do that without YOU.' I am a part.

I still believe in conversation: to see the other; to see myself. From the dynamic of authentic conversation, it is possible to be a part of creating the 'not yet.'

Today I want to add that increasingly I have no clue as to where 'we' are going. The human conundrum intensifies as we repeat mistakes with a new intensity; war ever present, intense cruelty, a vacuous political conversation. For me, there is nothing that is not 'political,' defined for me as that which creates our corporate wellbeing – and if that isn't 'spiritual,' what is? Who knows where I will be tomorrow, but what I do know is that silence is really important to me.

'Anybody who has paid attention to their inner life of prayer or read history books surely recognises that life and love are always cumulative, growing, and going somewhere that is always new and always more.'[8]

Peter

When I was ten, I had a teacher who liked to challenge us. One week, she asked us to write an essay on 'God.' My mum kept a copy of what I wrote, and I still remember the opening words: 'Some people think that God's home is the church. I disagree. I think God is everywhere. I am writing this essay with God.'

As a child and as a teenager, formal religion played little part in my life. I rarely went to church, and my mum pulled me out of Sunday school after a couple of weeks when the teacher began to talk about hell. Looking back, though, I can see how my parents' spirituality helped to shape my own beliefs.

My dad was dismissive of what he called 'churchianity.' He had spent more than half of his life in India, which had influenced his outlook. I remember, as a teen, having conversations with him about reincarnation. My mum had been raised as a Catholic in Poland. Shortly after moving to England, and while I was still in my pram, she had the first of a small number of mystical experiences where she felt, at the core of her being, the Oneness of all things. I ended up in a secondary school where the motto was 'serve and obey', where the teachers called us by our surnames, and where academic and sporting excellence seemed to be all. Competition and conformity, rather than co-operation and free-thinking, were the order of the day. My time at school was characterised by not fitting in. I often had the sense of not quite belonging in this world. I left school at eighteen with a string of A-levels (religious studies among them) and GCSEs, but with my confidence on the floor and very little self-worth.

My twenties were a time of slowly rebuilding my confidence and rediscovering who I was as an individual. Getting a job and being relatively successful at work, plus founding and running a national sports association, were stepping stones and bolstered my self-reliance, but on a social level I still struggled. I had little interest in 'small talk,' in superficial relationships, drinking, or going to clubs. My sporadic attempts at trying to conform myself to the world were invariably unsuccessful and left me feeling more of an outsider than ever.

By that time, my mum's work as an astrologer had morphed into an interest in spirituality and counselling, and she was training to be a psychosynthesis psychotherapist (psychosynthesis is a spiritual approach). She had an ever-growing collection of spiritual books and cassette programmes in her library and, at some point – around the age of twenty-five, when I left home – I began to borrow them. One of the first I read, which had a big impression on me, was Wayne Dyer's *You'll See It When You Believe It*. When I read about Oneness, Spiritual Reality, and the connectedness of all things, something stirred within me.

My late twenties and early thirties were a pivotal time in my journey. While I found inspiration in the words of Wayne Dyer and others, I longed for deeper connection with other people. I wanted to be part of a community where I could continue my spiritual journey alongside others.

With some trepidation, I went along to my local church. My initial experiences were positive – people were welcoming, and the preaching about our responsibility to the environment echoed my views. Encouraged by family, I signed up to do the Alpha course they were offering. Alpha is billed as an 'opportunity to explore the meaning of life.' What I soon found was that the course attempted to provide ready-made answers, at least at the church I attended. It presented a particular 'take' on Christianity. The emphasis seemed to be on belief, on assenting to certain intellectual propositions about Jesus and about God. Leaving aside that those propositions didn't make much sense to me, I struggled with why God would be so concerned with our intellectual beliefs. Surely how we lived our lives was more important? The final straw was the notion that, if we didn't believe 'the right' things, fire and brimstone awaited us. Hell as a physical place was implied at this course, and referred to more explicitly in a fiery sermon I recall from a female preacher at my mum's Baptist church. In response to a question I posed at the course, even Gandhi may not have been 'saved.' Something inside me revolted. 'God is Love' we were told in the Bible that people seemed to want to take so literally. If that was true, then how could He send anyone to Hell? An inner knowing told me it couldn't be so.

Put off from the Anglican and Baptist churches, I wondered if there might be a more open-minded, inclusive faith community where I could continue my seeking. Might other denominations be less rigid? I went on the Religion and Ethics section of the BBC website (now archived) and, when I read about Quakers, I found myself nodding to each bullet point. The way we live our lives is more important than what we believe. Yes. Everyone can have a direct personal relationship with God. Yes.

There is something of God in every person. Three times yes!

With enthusiasm rather than trepidation, I went along to Quaker Quest, the Quaker equivalent of Alpha, at Friends House in Euston, London. The topic for one of the sessions was 'Quakers and Christianity.' Three Friends (as Quakers are also known) shared their own personal experience. When someone in the audience asked if they considered themselves to be Christian, one of the speakers said 'Yes' (and explained why), the second replied 'No' (again with an explanation), and the third responded with a question: 'Well, it depends on what you mean by Christian.' This, I felt, was the home I had been looking for.

I began attending Quaker meetings, taking like a duck to water to the silent worship (although part of me missed the music of some of the more upbeat – and more theologically palatable – hymns they sang in church). After about four years, I decided to become a member of the Quakers – an outer commitment of an inner faith.

I came to see Friends as my spiritual basecamp, from which I could continue to explore other spiritual ideas. For a few years, the Progressive Christianity movement appealed to me. I loved Marcus Borg's *The Heart of Christianity*, in which he explained the difference between faith as belief, and faith as trust, which, he argued, was closer to the intended meaning of the word 'belief' as used in the gospels. I even hosted my own ecumenical house-group for those on the fringes of the church. Over time, though, my interest in theological questions began to wane –

whether or not there was a bodily resurrection, whether Jesus was born of a virgin... I'd come to a place where, either way, it was no longer important to my faith.

Another beacon on my journey was the Conversations with God books by Neale Donald Walsch, not so much for what they said in themselves (though I agreed with most if not all of it), but for their affirmation, shared by Quakers, that God, Spirit, Higher Self – call it what we like – can communicate with every one of us. Revelation didn't suddenly stop 1600 years ago, or whenever the canon of scripture was agreed. And not only that God can communicate with us, but that He/She/It does. The only question is, do we listen? Do we allow that Voice to be heard?

In 2006, my dad died. That same summer, I was in the process of switching roles at work and moving house. I was having second thoughts about the house move and felt paralysed, not knowing what to do. Reassurance came in the form of my own personal conversations with God, or dialogues with my Higher Self as I prefer to call them. I sat in silent reflection for a time and, when it felt right, took up a pen. I wrote a question and, without thinking, words would come to answer it, sometimes saying things or using language which, in everyday conversation or writing, I wouldn't think or use. Words flowed through me that didn't seem to be from me. It's a practice I've continued, on and off, ever since.

Two further experiences stand out for me. After four or five years as a Quaker, I returned to Quaker Quest in Euston, this time as one of the speakers. Once again, as it had been back at primary school, the topic was God. I don't recall what I said, but I remember speaking from the heart. Something must have resonated with at least one person in the audience because he approached me with the suggestion of my writing a short book for other Quakers around the same theme. The book emerged over a few months and, as with my earlier dialogues, it was more a case of allowing words to come through me than of thinking my own way around the subject and deciding what I wanted to say. Grounded in silence, I began with an idea for a chapter, and offered the invitation, 'Speak to me about Truth,' or 'Speak to me about "Simplicity",' or whatever the theme was.

Over the years, reinforced by my experience of writing the booklet, through daily quiet time, and long-term engagement with *A Course in Miracles*, I've come to believe, profoundly, in the Oneness of God and of all that is. God is not a being to be believed in or not, but Being Itself, Eternal Reality, That Which Is.

While I used to struggle with the idea of Jesus' divinity, I no longer do. I now see us all as spiritual beings (or, more accurately, as parts of the same Spiritual Essence, since God has one Son, not many). The difference between Jesus and you and me is not that he was divine, and we are not, but rather in the degree of his awareness of his own and everyone's divinity. Jesus remembered Who He Is, ('Before Abraham was, I am') and Who We All Are. For as long as I identify myself as solely my body, I perceive myself as separate and different from others. The commandment that I love my neighbour as myself appears fanciful and unattainable. However, when I recognise that shared Essence that is in both my neighbour and me, I begin to appreciate that what unites far exceeds the surface differences. In a sense, my neighbour is my Self.

I have experienced over and over that when I show kindness to another, I feel joy as though I were the recipient of the gift. Conversely, when I'm unkind, or if I judge another in some way, my own self contracts.

Perhaps the closest I have come to a peak experience of Oneness was in this last month. I awoke at 1 am with the thought, 'If Jesus were to attend a Quaker meeting, what would he say?' For the next three hours, I had an experience of communicating with God, with Spirit, with my True Self. Words came, but not many. Most of this experience was felt. My questions were answered by an inner knowing, a sense of peace that didn't need to be confined by words. At times in my life, I've felt lonely. In those moments, I knew that I was not alone; that I needed nothing; that all I could ever want, I already Am.

Voices of Inspiration

Both of these biographers had experienced a disruption of their originally faith, and this for some can be a difficult time. However, very often, new life-giving inspiration arrives that animates our lives and leads to a different and broader faith beyond former limitations.

'Humanity today yearns for a bigger picture than our currently subsumed perceptions, which entangle us in webs of religious minimalism. We yearn to reclaim the deep, primal sacred story of our evolving universe; of planet Earth as our cosmic home; in the diverse and magnificent array of life-forms around us; in the largely untold story of the evolution of spiritual consciousness within humanity itself; and, finally, in the contemporary desire to create a one-world family characterised by love, justice, peace and liberation.'[1] Diarmuid O'Murchu

Tim

My journey from being a committed Roman Catholic and a Catholic priest to being a searcher of no fixed religious address can be told in the story of a little boy who once upon a time was born in a magnificent castle. The castle was surrounded by woods and was very beautiful and very old. It was safe and could keep out intruders. Its massive stone walls were firmly built. It was clean inside, warm in winter and cool in summer. It was dry and kept out the rain and gales that swept across the woods and hammered at its walls. It had a good community spirit and most of the people who lived there were good people. Each had their place and knew what they had to do. The castle was well ordered and efficiently run. From its ramparts one could look out over the moat and the woods outside towards the faraway hills.

The little boy who was born in this castle grew up to be an active member of its community. When he was young he would often stand on the walls and watch the people who lived in the woods outside the castle, and gaze at the distant hills, and wonder what lay on the other side. When he grew up he enjoyed being part of the expeditions into the woods and came to realise that the people outside the castle were just like those inside it. He enjoyed being with these people and being closer to nature than he could be inside the castle. Although he enjoyed living in the castle and had many friends there, he gradually came to feel that the castle had become a prison for him and that he seemed to be more at home outside its walls. He knew he had to leave.

So, he went to live with the people in the woods. At times he missed the castle, the work he had done there and his friends and sometimes even envied their security. When he looked back at the castle, it seemed so small compared the vast woods and hills

– it seemed to have been placed there rather than having grown there like the trees. And the hills and trees were much older than the castle. The woods were not always safe, and he never knew if something would unexpectedly jump out at him. There were no walls in the woods, just vegetation which people could pass through easily. He would often get muddy, cold, and wet and became very aware of the changing weather and seasons. He soon discovered that the paths through the woods were not always clear, because at times he could not see very far ahead, though from time to time he would glimpse open fields or mountain peaks in the distance. He made many friends on his journeys and met many fellow travellers. Some of them had ideas he could not always agree with, and others were very odd or seemed to have even less idea of where they were going than he did. The castle had a deep moat of still water, but in the wood, there were meandering streams of running water. The castle had a plan of its layout but there was no such thing for the wood. If he looked down when living in the castle, he saw stone floors or man-made carpets; in the wood he saw the living earth. When he had looked up from the castle, he had seen the sky and stars and now in the wood when he looked up, he could see the same sky and stars, and he realised that everyone could see the same sky and stars wherever they were. He had been so sure of where he was while inside the castle but now he was not so sure. Sometimes he would sing the old Negro spiritual 'I wonder while I wander, and I wander while I wonder.'

I loved being a priest. I had been fortunate to have studied in Rome during the years of the Second Vatican Council and so had a ringside seat for that memorable event, which seemed to me to let common sense into the church. I was gripped by its broad vision of the church being an ally of all people of good will, its radical ecumenical openness and its portrayal of the church as primarily a community and not an institution. When I returned to England, I always had superiors who gave me my head, as a curate, in teaching theology in Allen Hall seminary, by Cardinal Basil Hume as one of his Vicars General and as a parish priest. Above all I was aware of the privilege of meeting and working with so many good, holy and inspiring people and to have the humbling privilege of being invited by so many to share their intimate moments of joy or suffering or decision. As a priest, I was never able to accept some aspects of the church such as its teaching on birth control, its refusal to allow the clergy to marry, or to ordain women as priests. Above all I was dismayed by the autocratic rule of Pope John Paul II, which seemed to be backtracking on the vision of Vatican II with an obsession with doctrinal orthodoxy and repeated assertions that other Christian churches and religions were 'defective in faith.'

I could probably have lived with these reservations, but deeper issues about my Christian beliefs had begun to surface. One was that I could no longer accept the (Catholic) Christian claim to have the fullness of truth. Increasingly I came to believe that there are many ways up the spiritual mountain and Catholicism was just one among many such ways. And like all religions, it is a human construction with all the strengths and weaknesses of any human construction. This led to an erosion of my belief in the fundamental Christian doctrine that Jesus is the only and universal saviour and the unique Son of God. I had come to see him as one among many great spiritual teachers.

In addition, I found that I could no longer reconcile innocent human suffering with my image of a personal, loving and all-powerful god. Either this 'god' is a sadist who permits indescribable suffering to happen or he is not all-powerful and cannot prevent it. And I also discovered that I no longer believed in the Christian notion of redemption, which appeared to me to be about placating a vengeful god who demands the sacrificial death of the innocent man Jesus as the price of our salvation. This led me to dread celebrating the Eucharist: I could celebrate it as the community's memorial and thanksgiving for Jesus, but not as a sharing in the sacrifice of Jesus which Catholicism claims it to be.

So, I reached a point where I could no longer in good conscience call myself a Christian or a Catholic. And most importantly, Catholics have a right to expect their priests to share their basic faith. That is why they share their confidences with them and go to confession. For me to have continued as a priest while not sharing their basic beliefs would have been to betray these good people and to have been dishonest with them.

So, I left the castle. For a long time, I felt very alone spiritually and would often wonder if I was off the wall and whether there was anyone else out there who felt as I did. But it was during this time that a wise lady said to me that my image of god had to die if I was to move forward. She was right. My image of god as a supernatural personal being had died. I was in a god-vacuum where everything seemed to scream at me that there was no god.

But gradually I came to realise that while the Christian image of a personal god no longer made sense to me, there is a reality in which I believed – a reality which is greater than we are, which we do not invent, and which is ultimately incomprehensible. The image of this reality as the Mystery of Being and the Creative Energy in all existence, rather than a personal god, did have meaning for me. And I began to find others who were making similar spiritual journeys, and over time became involved in networks such as CANA, Quo Vadis, The Wrekin Trust, Greenspirit, and the local Inter-Faith Forum. These open, affirming and accepting communities, which draw on the wisdoms of all the religions and all humanity, have now become my spiritual home and my community. I have been greatly helped by discovering such writers as Diarmuid O'Murchu (especially his *Reclaiming Spirituality*), Adrian Smith (especially his *God Shift*) and above all Cyprian Smith's *The Way of Paradox* on the writings of Meister Eckhart where I came across the magical words that 'If the eye of the heart were fully open, we would see that contraries are all contained finally in an all-embracing unity.' This was my Eureka moment. because it seemed to hold the key to getting beyond the impasse of our 'either/or' human and religious divisions and it also led me to understand that at the heart of the Great Mystery of Being is relationship – as Martin Buber said, 'All real living is meeting. Here is the cradle of real life.'

How do I now relate to the Catholicism of my birth? I continue to be inspired by the many good and loving Christians, and those of other faith traditions, who are obviously nourished by their religious beliefs. I still draw on much of the wisdom of the Catholic tradition, especially its notion of the sacramentality of all creation, beauty, creativity and above all love as being the signs and symbols of the divine presence. But I find attending Christian worship difficult, because I feel such an outsider and find myself editing out the many bits that have no meaning for me. This is hardly inducive to a worshipping or peaceful frame of mind! And I must confess that many of the pronouncements of official Christianity seem so petty and irrelevant (and sometimes plain wrong) compared to today's huge issues of violence, poverty and over-population, let alone the ecological threats to our planet. I find it sad, if not repellent, that the Anglican Communion is tearing itself apart over women and gay bishops and that in Catholicism there are interminable divisive arguments about the liturgy and doctrine as if these issues were what Jesus was about, while many open-minded Catholic theologians and activists constantly have to look over their shoulders to see if and when the Vatican will crack down on them.

So where does my inspiration come from now?

Inspiration is a good word because it suggests the Spirit within us and our spirituality which, as Adrian Smith says, is 'that aspect of our nature which awakens us to wonder, gives our lives meaning and calls us to our higher selves, and is usually expressed as a relationship with the transcendent.'[1,2] For me the transcendent reality, that great Mystery of Being and Creative Energy in all being, which many call 'god,' is beyond our comprehension and provokes a sense of wonder, acceptance and gratitude. 'Mystery is a gift to be enjoyed, not a problem to be solved.'[3] It is in relationships that I can catch glimpses of the nature of this great Mystery of Being out of the corner of my eye. I believe that relationship is the basis of all reality. It is the nature of the cosmos itself at the macro/galactic, the micro/sub-atomic, the natural and human levels because everything which exists is interconnected and related to everything else.

It is not surprising that many religions have described the divine as interpersonal relationship including the Christian notion of the Trinity with its idea of one god in three persons. And relationship reminds us that reality is not 'either/or' nor meant to be a dualistic clash of opposites whether it be the spiritual against the material, the feminine against the masculine or this religion against that religion. But rather it is a both/and reality with both unity and also diversity held together by respect, acceptance and love.

It has been rightly said that nothing destroys relationship more than wanting to dominate, and that is why I believe so passionately that we have to stop dominating nature, not just to avoid global catastrophe, but in order to be true to the Great Mystery of Being itself. As in the religious sphere, I am inspired by Jean Vanier's words that 'too much inter-religious dialogue begins with theology and spirituality and in a comparison of belief systems and so gets stuck. Better to ask "What does it mean to be a human being and how do human beings grow? What is freedom, what is human maturity?" Religious beliefs can be tackled later after the discovery of a shared humanity and the mutual acceptance of the other.'[4] Or as Bede Griffiths urged, one should be true to one's own tradition but go beyond its limitations to a greater Oneness.

My spiritual journey has been full of the unexpected and seems to have come a long way so far. I share with so many others great fears for the future of our planet, almost a despair that poverty will ever be solved or that violence will ever cease. In the religious sphere, I am disturbed by the rise of divisive religious fundamentalism. But I am also inspired and given hope by what is unmistakably a new awareness and a new consciousness that is bursting out everywhere in different movements and networks, which cross the boundaries of culture and religion in seeking unity while honouring diversity – whether in the ecological, social or religious spheres. It is giving new life to ancient wisdoms and giving us new insights. I have no doubt that we are being called into a new age. It's an exciting and challenging age to enter and at times it is daunting. Now in my seventies, I am grateful to have lived long enough to be part of this crucial step in our human story.

Petra

When I came across Mathew Fox's work on the creation-centred tradition of Christianity in my late thirties, it gave me a much broader vision of what Christianity was at its origins and enabled me to relate to it again. I had left the non-conformist chapel I belonged to in my mid-teens, since I found the services boring at that point and felt that a choice was being presented between living in the body and being Christian. At that point I chose my body.

Since Donald Reeves was providing a place at St James's church, Piccadilly, where creation spirituality could be experimented with, I began to go to the services there and discovered that there were some women in ministry (before they could be priests) who were providing very healing approaches. This meant I developed a different understanding of Christianity. Donald's own very creative and maverick ministry also opened up large spaces for people and connected with the great issues of the time, especially growing inequality in the 1980s. The encouragement to ask questions and not leave your mind outside the door helped the formal services to feel inclusive. The extent of involvement of laypeople was also very impressive.

I was also encouraged by the work of the Anglican Industrial Chaplains, who were the most helpful people around when I was involved in unemployment campaigns, since they didn't impose their own agendas on people. When I had a period of unemployment and lack of money, I was very encouraged by the public statements that Bishops David Sheppard and David Jenkins made on the national stage, which helped counteract the feeling of increasing marginalisation of poor people when benefits were cut.

For me it was the fact that Donald Reeves entrusted the work of taking forward creation spirituality in the UK to me that enabled me to have a clear role at St James's and some resources to enable us to experiment with courses, workshops and creative forms of liturgy. I have been a member of St James's ever since, becoming confirmed and baptised in 1998.

Since then, my involvement has varied greatly over time, but there have always been creative initiatives taking place, and it has always been a supportive place for individuals in trouble despite the very scattered congregation. Relationships at the church helped me greatly both when my husband was very ill and then died, and when I had surgery on both my knees. At times I have felt I had one foot in and one foot out, but I've always maintained my involvement. I now admire the courageous leadership at St James's under Lucy Winkett, who sticks her neck out for important and sometimes controversial causes, and often does this through creative media such as art installations and sculptures, which engage people's interest.

In the last year, I have had two powerful experiences that brought about a further deepening of trust (faith being a more traditional word for this). One was on All Souls Day at St James's and the other on Passion Sunday at St David's Cathedral in West Wales. In both, I felt mind letting go under the unbearable pressure of the suffering it was focused on, and which can't be understood with the mind, but felt the great strength of the tradition, the beauty of the buildings, the inspiration of the choirs, and the stability of the clergy and servers as providing a very secure and lasting holding that is able to be there now and in the future for the unbearable pain that is a part of many lives.

My faith and spiritual practice now

I believe that the Holy Spirit is present in the liturgies at St James's and that the traditional wording of the liturgy – although much of it is not meaningful to many of those who attend – doesn't prevent a real spiritual presence there, which I sometimes sense directly, often through music, or through the movement round the church and gathering as one body around the altar.

In order to have inclusively worded liturgies, we have Journeying Together meetings monthly, which enable a group of us to connect, explore the themes that are of interest, and to celebrate life events and support one another when there is illness or other forms of trouble.

In addition, I have a daily practice of journaling; of going through the Shibashi Tai Chi/Qi Gong form; and ending the day with 4 Qi Gongfour qi gong movements and some practices from

David Steindl-Rast's Gratitude and Sufficiency course that I participated in this year. I am just beginning a further study of Loch Kelly's practice of open-hearted awareness and will be trying out the meditations he suggests.

Books are certainly a source of nourishment. Circle dance and Skinner Release Dance were also important, but I have needed to give those up since having a hip fracture. Visits to the countryside and sea are important. Singing and attending inspiring concerts are also very nourishing. Two or three times a year I also attend Sacred Thread workshops for women, involving the labyrinth, many other creative media, and some meditations.

How my present spirituality relates to traditional Christianity

I am in tune with some contemporary versions of Christianity, e.g., Richard Rohr, Cynthia Bourgeault, Matthew Fox, Thomas Keating, which suggest that much of what we consider traditional Christianity is a version brought in as a result of the influence of the Roman Empire and has been out of touch with the mystical traditions. Contemplatives such as Julian of Norwich, Hildegard of Bingen and Meister Eckhart are formative influences.

What inspiration or vision is moving me forward?

I still find the vision set out in Matthew Fox's *Original Blessing* inspiring, and agree with him that we need to give birth to the images that arise at a deep level within us, and to be in tune with all four paths (savouring creation, letting pain be pain, following our creative inspirations, and contributing to the transformation of society for the benefit of all, including the earth, and all parts of nature). I am pursuing this vision through Living Spirituality Connections and through our partnership with Spirit of Peace. I believe that we need to experience the presence of the sacred within the everyday, and listen for what the spirit is saying (a phrase that is used in church every Sunday after the first reading). I experience a flow of energy from the universe through us humans, if we are open to it. Practices like Qi gong help us to experience cosmic cycles of energy.

We need to live as though all of life is interconnected, and respect the diversity within life as well as the unity of life. Everyone has the potential to listen to deep sources of wisdom within them. Living as though the earth matters is vital for the future of humanity. New patterns emerge and gather energy within the life of the world and we need to trust them and help bring them to birth where we discern that they are from a sacred source.

In what ways is my understanding and practice shifting towards a more universal spirituality?

Since coming across Matthew Fox's work, I have found his description of the deep underground river that has many wells a good description of the underlying unity behind all manifestations of faith. I don't want to move towards forms of

☐

worship that cancel out all traditions. I believe that this universal great spirit can operate through and change existing religious forms, where there is openness.

Voices of Unity

'Many groups are now sensing a call to use their energies in working together for a world in which all people can flourish, to be at the service of humanity as a whole. This awareness is felt most clearly in the growing numbers of people who are finding in Christ's teachings the call to become more fully human and deeply engaged with co-creating a new world.'[1] Living Spirituality Connections website.

Jill

Beginnings

My childhood was secure, and my parents exercised a strong moral code and social conscience. They believed and practised the principle of loving thy neighbour and have spent a lifetime serving others. However, religion played no part in family life. I did, however, attend the Methodist Church in my teens (largely because of its excellent youth club), attended church regularly, taught in the Sunday School and became confirmed. This experience awakened my spiritual sense but I gained little enlightenment and was very uncomfortable with the doctrines I was expected to believe. However, this was the beginning of a strong intuitive drive for connection with the Spirit, which has persisted throughout my life, despite consistent discouragement from the Church.

My spiritual search continued, somewhat erratically, at university where I studied the biological sciences. Positive spiritual experiences included the discovery of Teilhard de Chardin, Anglican Choral Services in beautiful Chapels, and having my one and only numinous experience. Not so positive was the pressure put on me by my fundamentalist peers to become a 'Committed Christian', largely through threats of hellfire and damnation! Not only was I completely unable to accept the traditional Christian doctrines, conceptually I also struggled to believe in free will at all when my scientific training appeared to indicate that we were all determined by the complex interplay between our genes and environment.

On balance, I left University no further forward spiritually, and this continued throughout subsequent years. My spiritual awareness was largely submerged under the struggle to survive both materially and emotionally during professional social work training, challenging work in education social work practice and management, an alcoholic partner in marriage, motherhood and divorce. I nevertheless felt impelled to keep searching, however unsuccessfully: I attended the local Anglican church regularly, prayed as best I could, and continued to read and debate... but my spiritual heart was not consoled or engaged by the form of Christianity to which I had access.

First Steps

However, in the attempt to cope with the trauma of my husband's alcoholism and its consequences, I found spiritual enlightenment and consolation unexpectedly elsewhere: in the Al-Anon Twelve Step Fellowship and in the principles of Reality Therapy built upon them (all summarised so well in the Serenity Prayer). In desperation, I was driven to stop busily trying to control the situation and I let go and trusted in God... Miracles followed! My ex-husband went voluntarily into treatment; and, in the fullness of time, also in answer to prayer, my beloved second husband appeared. And with it, our mutually beneficial spiritual dialogue began. He introduced me to Transcendental Meditation, which I practised for some time, and which provided the basis for my current Christian meditation practice.

Quantum Leap

But it was during our residence in Derbyshire in the 1990s that I took a quantum leap in spiritual understanding. There were several significant influences, a major one being the discovery of the spiritual guidance provided by M. Scott Peck in his seminal books. Another was joining the local Anglican church, where we attended a Christian Basics Course to learn about contemporary Christianity. We found that nothing had changed since our youth. The course and the church were evangelical, and we were told that being a Christian required literal belief in traditional doctrines, such as the Fall and substitutionary atonement. This was impossible for both of us. While still believing deeply that Jesus was a unique and outstandingly inspirational disclosure of a loving God, and wishing to continue to worship and serve God within a Christian framework, I could not believe that Jesus was the only, the complete, or the final disclosure of the divine. My naturally enquiring mind and eclectic reading have increasingly led me to question the exclusivity and supremacy of the orthodox Christian faith and the absolute and often literal truth asserted for the Bible and traditional Christian doctrines, many of which do not sit comfortably with biblical scholarship or contemporary scientific, psychological and historical knowledge. Unfortunately, such questioning was not welcomed by the church and we felt unable to voice our views. Despite this and remembering Lord Hailsham's dictum, 'Faith is an act of the will,' I felt impelled to make a personal and public act of commitment of faith, but I made this to God, not to Christian doctrines. Sadly, involvement in the life of the Church became increasingly difficult for both of us as we were expected to keep affirming the party line.

Two wonderful things then happened. First, we discovered the Omega Foundation, a Christian Contemplative Order near Bristol that practises a spirituality of the heart. It was at an Omega Insight retreat that I found the true starting point for my inner spiritual journey. I also found the answer to the free will question, namely that I am an open system and by opening my heart to God – Source of all Being – I am capable of a slow transformation towards greater wholeness and self-realisation. Rather surprisingly as a biologist, this was a revelation to me and made sense of my social work practice.

The Retreat leader assured us that whatever our personal perspective on Church doctrines, it could be voiced and would be respected. We were told of our capacity to experience intuitive insight giving us direct knowledge of God's truth and wisdom by opening our hearts directly to His loving spirit. More significantly for me, the leader spoke of the changing nature of much revealed truth and wisdom in response to our own deepening understanding and the changing context. At the final office of the Retreat I was happy and elated to be included as one of the People of God. I knew that I had found the right inner path and looked forward to moving deeper into the mystery however uncertain and difficult it might be.

Back to Church

However, the inner journey was not enough for me. Intuitively, I needed to earth my spiritual awareness and to be connected to a local spiritual community where the collective spirit is grounded in the world and where I could share in serving that community. So, I returned to my local church and with my husband set up an unemployment project. I did not expect to find anyone there with whom to share my inner journey or my perspective on the faith, but the second wonderful thing happened. We discovered a remarkable group of church members who not only shared our reservations with the church's approach but – joy oh joy – met monthly at a brilliantly led Study Group to share these and to study contemporary ideas and faith frameworks. I was thrilled to be introduced to Keith Ward's *A Vision to Pursue*, books by John Spong, Richard Holloway, Don Cupitt and others. We attended conferences organised by the Sea of Faith and the Modern Church People's Union. I had at last found a satisfactory intellectual framework for my Christian faith, which allowed belief with integrity.

New Kinds of Spiritual Practice

With my intellect satisfied, I could travel on my inner journey wholeheartedly and with the support of several of the Group members who had been on the path for years. We met at 7 a.m. on Monday morning for reflection and meditation and breakfast afterwards: a wonderful way to start the week. I was also introduced to the experiential work of the San Francisco School of Psychological Studies, which understood the depth psychology at the heart of spirituality. A seminal book for me was *The Choicemaker* by Howes and Moon. I attended several group sessions in Sheffield, in which we were invited to act out characters in the parables and to share our insights. These sessions introduced me to the experience of hunting for the treasure within. It was at this time that I discovered Psychosynthesis – a psychology with a soul – which offers a model of theory and practice that made total sense of the 'treasure hunt' as the driving purpose of the spiritual journey. As well as the conscious ego-self, it posits a Higher or God Self in the higher unconscious, which is at the heart of the personality and is the place of connection with God. The journey is about integrating all parts of the personality and seeking connection with the Higher Self. For some people this connection is sudden (experienced as a conversion or numinous experience); for me and most people it is a gradual process of spiritual awakening. My husband and I also attended an Omega retreat on Psychosynthesis, where we practised several exercises to develop our inner creative potential.

Discovered by CANA

Having discovered this relevant and inspiring approach to Christianity, I became increasingly amazed that the Church had not shared this with its members and with the world at large. Not only was the voice of 'progressive' Christians not being heard within the Church, the spiritual needs of the community at large were being ignored. I had no doubt that if non-church goers had heard of this contemporary approach to the faith, many would have found it of great value to them. So, I wrote an article for the parish magazine about it. It was rejected. The Omega Foundation kindly published it for me under the title Fling Wide the Gates. Among the many who responded, Adrian Smith, a member of the CANA Core Group, invited me to join, which I did, so beginning a new adventure on my journey.

At the time, I was struggling to write my framework of

beliefs to see how they compared with the traditional beliefs being taught at the Alpha course I was attending. We discussed this with the Core Group at the CANA retreat on Iona, and decided to work on an emergent 'creed' together. I became deeply involved with other CANA members as we shared our beliefs in the production of the CANA publication *Exploring Ways Forward for Christianity in the 21st Century*, and in convening the first Round Table of like-minded groups.

Travelling with fellow CANA members has been joyous and challenging. It has opened my heart and mind to so many new possibilities. I am now willing to consider ideas previously I would have discounted: reincarnation, nature spirits, astrology, psychic phenomena… But more than this, it has helped me beyond measure to enjoy travelling into the mystery with uncertainty, to cherish diversity and to travel in trust and hope.

A New Church Experience

Soon after this, we moved south for family reasons and joined our traditional parish church, where our approach to the faith was discounted. Although I joined the choir and was involved in supporting the homeless, I stayed on the fringes of church life. However, I found some fellow spirits in the town and we formed a Spirituality Group for people of any faith (mostly Christian) or none, which meets monthly to support each other. This has been a source of spiritual growth and strength to us all as we sought to share our exciting new understanding of the faith in our churches. We arranged for Bishop Jack Spong to give a public lecture on A New Christianity for a New World, which was a sell-out and has triggered many open discussions on the faith within the local church community. Also, I was allowed to initiate a small church group to explore aspects of the faith in an atmosphere of open enquiry. I now feel more at home in the church and can make a greater contribution to church life at last.

There were two important triggers for my inner journey during this period. The first was practising the Ignatian Exercises under the supervision of a Spiritual Director who was remarkable not only in his discernment and non-directive guidance, but in his total acceptance of my radically different framework of understanding from his own evangelical position. For the first time in my life, I experienced a deep inner awareness of God's love and forgiveness. I felt an enormous burden of guilt lift from my shoulders. I also learned to hear the inner voice and gained insight into my own motivations. I became able to discriminate between my true vocation – what I truly wanted to do, which brought life to me and to others – and what I felt I ought to do, which often brought resentment and negativity all round.

This issue became of particular importance in another crucial strand in my spiritual awareness, namely my deep affinity with nature and in particular my fellow creatures. I believe passionately in the intrinsic value of all living beings, and view human beings as just one particular strand in the web of life. Despite this passion and my grief at humanity's destruction of our living world, I still struggle to develop the deep inner ecological awareness and sense of cosmic belonging, which will lead me to want, not just feel that I ought, to live a fully sustainable life. I founded an eco-group in my town, and we monitored and sought to reduce our ecological impact. We found that our willingness to change our lifestyles for the good of the earth was limited. I realised that 'living lightly' entailed the selfless love that Jesus showed, and required a deep spiritual transformation, which I am still struggling to foster. In an attempt to make a deeper connection with nature, my husband and I attended Findhorn for the Experience Week. It helped, but I still have a long way to go.

While I practise my spirituality largely within the Christian tradition, I am open to the insights and practices of other faiths, since I believe that they all offer valid paths up the mountain. I have found aspects of the Hindu and Buddhist traditions of particular value in enriching my spiritual understanding and awareness. My husband and I are very committed to interfaith work and were involved for several years with the International Interfaith Centre in Oxford.

Present Faith and Practice

My present faith is based on reinterpreting Christianity in light of modern understanding of an evolving cosmos, of which we are an integral part. This evolution is powered and guided by an underlying creative, loving life force, which I call 'God.' Human beings are variously conscious of the cosmic life force urging us to evolve to wholeness, higher consciousness and selflessness and to become one with God. God is a mystery, but deep in our consciousness lies our Higher or God Self, which is the Place where we can transcend our ego-selves, become self-less and experience 'the love and voice of God.' Most of us only make a partial and intermittent connection with God, but Jesus lived all the time in full communion with Him and expressed God's love and wisdom in His life. The purpose of my spiritual journey is to become more in touch with God, and Jesus is my model for living. I believe in a fully inclusive Christianity in which the overarching principle is Love. The model that most nearly matches my understanding is that of Creation Spirituality, promoted in the UK by GreenSpirit. I value the scriptures and teachings of the Church as treasure houses of spiritual wisdom, but I interpret them metaphorically, not literally.

My practice today consists of daily Christian meditation, and contemplation on various wisdom texts (including the Bible and latterly the *Gospel of Thomas* by Hugh McGregor Ross), and occasional Ignatian exercises (under the guidance of Gerard Hughes' books). I attend my local church, usually at the early service. CANA events, including worshipping with the Grail Liturgy, are important, as are the events organised by the Progressive Christianity Network and the Centre for Radical Christianity in Sheffield. I could go on. My spiritual nourishment also comes from the books I read, particularly those by Thomas

Berry, Brian Swimme, Fritjof Kapra, and Diarmuid O'Murchu, and from music, poetry and nature.

My vision and Inspiration

What keeps me travelling on this difficult journey? My twin visions and the companionship of fellow visionaries. My first concerns the whole world: it envisages that the small-scale eco-spiritual developments now bubbling up all over the world coalesce to create a just, sustainable, and peaceful world, so that humanity can cooperate fully with God in the future unfolding.

My other vision is a more local one. I dream that our local UK 'churches' will become spiritual centres welcoming equally anyone who seeks spiritual nourishment, whatever their religion or none. That these centres become loving hearts of the community, showing love to all who come to them and working to alleviate need, promote justice and peace.

My inspiration are all those people who are doing Christ's work today, wherever they are found inside or outside churches. They are the ones who, by sacrificing themselves, will save the world.

Update

Towards Universalism

Since first writing about my spiritual journey in the Christian tradition, I have continued to explore further the mystery of faith. This has entailed reading writings of very progressive Christians who are exploring further beyond the earlier liberal boundaries, such as Gretta Vosper, Minister in the United Church of Canada; the Australian Christian theologian and author, Val Webb, science graduate and PhD in theology. They both spoke at public meetings that the Progressive Christianity Network (Abingdon) helped to organise, as part of the respective speakers' UK tours. Both gave their audiences the opportunity to start thinking well outside the Christian box.

Gretta Vosper is an atheist who has no belief in a theistic, supernatural being. Her work bridges progressive Christianity and atheism, exploring beyond the boundaries of Christian thought. Her seminal book *With or Without God* argues for a post-Christian church where the way we live is more important than what we believe. Gretta conducted a Sunday service in the Chapel at Somerville College, Oxford, which, although drawing on some Christian material, was expressed largely in day to day language, which, unlike traditional churches, would therefore have been accessible to the non-churchgoing public.

Val Webb, author of *In Defence of Doubt: An Invitation to Adventure*, spoke in celebration of doubt as a catalyst on the faith journey.

Essentially, all these new lines of thinking and practice point to the increasing need for people to find alternative ways to find meaning and spiritual support in their lives, beyond the doctrinal rigidities of the past.

As well as finding fellow explorers in the Christian

tradition, I have been involved in interfaith work. Here I have been increasingly aware of the commonalities in the spiritual journeys of people of all faiths and none, albeit expressed in different forms due to different cultural origins. It has been particularly striking to discover that they all fulfil the same two purposes: first, through meditation or prayer to seek connection with God (however, understood) for peace, guidance and comfort; and second, to belong to a group of people who are working not only for their own mutual care and support but also and most importantly for the common good.

It is therefore in the two practices of meditation and prayer, and social action, that people of all faiths (and none) come together. These universal practices underpin all forms of spirituality, including that of humanism: believers who meditate or pray seek connection with an external Higher Power; whereas humanists who meditate seek connection with such a power deep within themselves. As I understand it, humanists believe that this material world is all that exists, there is nothing else. Believers like myself are unable to accept this: my inner world of subjective consciousness tells of another domain of existence that I don't believe that scientists will explain. This is where the mysterious nature of reality lies. So, although I personally practise my spirituality within the Christian tradition, I am a universalist in my understanding that what is at the heart of all religious traditions is the same.

Magda

'Hear O Israel, The Lord our God, the Lord is One.' These words from The Shema in the Old Testament book of Deuteronomy have always spoken to me in a profound way. In many ways they capture something of my journey – Israel means 'he struggles with God,' and my journey has often involved the struggle to believe, even to survive en route to a deeper awareness of the Divine Oneness, and my changing understanding of what this might mean.

So here I am, on the Core Group of a network called CANA, attempting to work out quite how I got here! I was baptised an Anglican as an infant, then underwent adult baptism in a Free Independent Evangelical Church after a 'forced' conversion at 13 when a vigorous and enthusiastic preacher got me, the shy, wouldn't say boo to a goose teenager to accept Jesus Christ as my Saviour. I was officially born again but the inner reality felt different.

On that night of decision when I was told that I had passed from death to life in the space of a prayer, a rift opened up within me. Had my early faith been unreal? What felt more unreal was this ABC approach, accept, believe, commit (though I know it has been a valuable experience for countless Christians). This and other questions led me to the place where I attempt to 'live the questions' and even find answers, not always intellectual ones, more an inner sense of knowing, a way of being, a sense of wholeness within the reality of the Divine.

'Be patient towards all that is unsolved in your heart...
And the point is to live everything. Live the questions now.
Perhaps you will then gradually, without noticing it, live along
some distant day into the answer.'[2] (Rainer Maria Rilke, *Letters
to a Young Poet.*)

Perhaps on that night, so unforgettable and rather long
ago now, I was in one sense born again or entering the birth pangs
of a new way of being. That split in my spiritual 'psyche' is leading,
as I learn to listen to the Divine voice in life, in sacred texts, in
others, to a place of greater integration, and of a sense of
connectedness, within the sacred web of life.

As I write, I am sitting in a beautiful room in a
Benedictine Abbey, beneath a painting depicting The Road to
Emmaus, one of my favourite gospel stories. Jesus the Christ is
breaking the bread, and, in this act, he is recognised. That story
has become my story as I begin to recognise the presence of Christ
where previously I could not discern him, indeed in places I was
taught to believe he could not be present, and to find the bread of
spiritual nourishment in diverse places.

Recognising the Christ in this way has required a
breaking open, sometimes painful and traumatic, sometimes
gentle and joyful, as the shell of old limitations, beliefs and
certainties has been pulled apart and a new order has come into
place.

Two main spurs to awakening have been that both my
sense of inner reality and my outward experience of life failed to

match the words and understandings passed to me, and my propensity for asking questions and being surprised at the answers that emerged. Old certainties began to dissolve and many formulations I could no longer understand in the same way. There was isolation and loneliness as internally I felt more and more adrift from the beliefs and often the way of life of the groups I had felt so much a part of. The way sometimes seemed dark as a sense of unknowing enveloped me, yet even within the most difficult times something would 'crop-up' to guide me – a word that brought inklings of a new direction and fresh insights.

Sporadically, the right book would appear, or responding to a sense of inner guidance, I made a new discovery. Gradually I learnt to follow this sense of being directed, to trust the Spirit within this process, and to accept that whenever I was apparently in a cul-de-sac, if I waited, trusted and opened myself, the next step forward would be revealed. I began to discover that there were many others who had similar experiences, who were also waking up to a reality that is shaped by inclusiveness, oneness, connectedness, and a sense of Sacred Unity underlying creation, a growing mystical awareness. Following the guidance that seemed to come both from without and within but always underpinned by a gentle sense of 'rightness' has led me to two particular kinds of expressions of Christian spirituality. Perhaps rather appropriately, these came together in the place where I am writing.

It was here that I attended a meditation day led by Fr Adrian Smith, and through him discovered CANA. Also on that day, walking through the Abbey church, I stumbled into The Daily Offices, the chanting that seemed such a deep intimation of eternity, a portal into another dimension of existence, and left a glowing ember within, later becoming an important source of spiritual nourishment.

Through the Benedictine tradition, I discovered sources of inspiration and transformation such as spiritual direction/accompaniment (an old tradition, yet a process that has facilitated both this growing new awareness and a deeper connection to Christ for me). The Monastic tradition of Lectio Divina has provided a framework and tool for a much more heart-centred, contemplative way of coming to Sacred writings. Writers such as Thomas Merton, Hans Kung, Bede Griffiths, and a whole range of books, mainly Catholic in origin, not previously within my reach, became available to me, as well as the writings of Rumi, a Sufi mystic who has been an important influence. I felt drawn to the monastic ideal as a way of life expressing a total commitment to, and shaped by, the spiritual dimension of living. I developed a sense of connection to saints and their energy. Those who have set out before us can still influence us from the dimension of reality they exist in now.

CANA, whilst rooted in Christianity, has facilitated an exploration of the universal truths at the heart of all religion plus new ways of understanding and experiencing the Christ-event. I have found a more holistic and integrated approach that is deeply satisfying and more 'of a piece.' This was through concepts such as Christ consciousness, a greater recognition of the feminine (human and divine), spirituality not limited to a personal relationship with the divine but intimately concerned with our humanity, our relationships, the natural world, the way we think about the cosmos and our place in it.

Particularly valuable has been the experience of a synergistic way of working, which comes about when hierarchy is minimal, the contributions of all are valued, and each is connected to each other through atunement to 'the centre' rather than by position or status in a given structure.

Another growing source of inspiration is Middle Eastern spirituality. Having long experienced a strong sense of connection to the Jewish roots of Christianity, I am now becoming more acquainted with a wider understanding of the spirituality emerging from The Middle East. Some of this comes from an exploration of the Jewish and Aramaic Jesus, and from Sufi and other forms of prayer and meditation.

All of what I have written pales somewhat in comparison to the deep inner journey of the heart that is taking place in all of this. I hesitate to speak of such things, for in any case they can barely be expressed in words. I hesitate too, because my life hardly matches up to these experiences of Christ so powerfully shattering and yet life-giving. Living in the Light of these experiences and assimilating them is a long work in progress of the Spirit, which I hope that I may be able to cooperate with. Suffice it to say that the journey into my own heart has sometimes led to a place, which I experience as the heart of Christ, so immense, full of love, sorrow, joy and LIFE that I cannot live too close to it for very long. Through this I have come to a deeper experience of Mass/Eucharist as a potentially unifying celebration, which can transcend time and space through eternal love. I am saddened that too often our experience of it is quite the opposite. In this respect, the prayer of Paul for the Ephesians continues to be very significant to me:

'I pray that you, being rooted and established in love, may have power, together with all the saints, to grasp how wide and long and high and deep is the love of Christ, and to know this love that surpasses knowledge – that you may be filled to the measure of all the fullness of God.' *(Ephesians* 3.17-19)

I believe that love requires a synthesis of the non-dualism of union with God and the dualism of relationship with and within The Divine.

How does this relate to the New Awareness? I do not entirely know, except to say that as this journey of the heart has continued, so has my journey into the New Awareness. I recognise that I am but a novice in all this; many much larger souls have lived with a far greater realisation of the heart, both within and outside of Christianity. This piercing revelation of Christ does not appear to me to be quite the same as the experience of Oneness, but feels more creative and active. My sense at present is that one is an experience of something passive, the other active. Both my theology and experience are inadequate and partial. I believe that the Kingdom of God will be fully revealed when we, collectively and individually, arrive at the Sacred Whole.

The vision that energises my life is succinctly drawn by the late Benedictine monk Bede Griffiths, who has written much on topics such as the universal Christ and the marriage between Eastern and Western forms of spirituality:

'This is our destiny, to be one with God in a unity transcending all distinctions, and yet in which each individual being is found in his integral wholeness.'[3]

Beneath the chaos and violence of our times, I am becoming aware of growing numbers of people and networks who are living and working towards this vision from an inclusive perspective, living creatively with difference and the interplay between the old and the new. From this I see the development of spiritual centres, retreat houses, multi-faith community groups, etc., bound together more by common purpose than by statements of creed. I believe that there will be continued growth in groups like CANA, The Bede Griffiths Sangha, The worldwide Christian Meditation centre and other new consciousness movements, not just in Christianity but in other religions and in other areas of life.

Within the institutional church Lay movements, cell churches and what some are calling The New Monasticism will become increasingly important. The church is beginning to move beyond former boundaries and there are signs of renewal coming from an approach that might be described as contemplation in action. Conservatism and fundamentalism are also on the rise, many seeing these as a response to the uncertainties of the Post-modern era. I think there will be a huge evolutionary leap forward when both those who feel themselves to be in the new, and those whose approach is fundamentalist, stop being in opposition and seek to understand each other.

According to Yossi Klein Halevi, in one of my all-time favourite spiritual books, *At the Entrance to the Garden of Eden*, the Shema with which I opened this story can lead to 'radical monotheism.'

'If God is literally one, and all of creation is a projection of that unified will, then every living thing exists within the same organism, is in effect a cell in the divine 'body,' as mystics insist... so all love is ultimately self-love; all hatred, self-hate. For the radical monotheist, empathy is the only possible state of being. Human oneness isn't a philosophical notion or a moral imperative but simply a fact.'4

My meagre attempts to live this out lead me to accompany others spiritually, and involvement in networks like CANA, peace, justice and social work, interfaith and spiritual peace making. I believe that these involvements are an expression of working for The Kingdom of God. An awakening Christian, I am moving forward, living and working in hope of the time when all shall be brought together in unity and peace (which for me contains the idea of creative possibility, not just absence of strife), when that original SHALOM, from which the world was formed, shall prevail. Each time I recite the Shema I affirm my belief that each of us comes from and lives within the same divine source and are united by a bond which transcends our differences, whether we recognise and like it or not!

Update

Since writing the piece above, I have become increasingly aware of a shift underway in spirituality today, one which I feel myself to be part of. From a heaven-focussed spirituality that placed emphasis on transcending the world and the human condition, there is a yearning and movement towards one which includes all of life on planet Earth. The focus is on the interconnectedness of all life and deeper engagement with humanity, and an appreciation of our place within the whole cosmos.

'Collective salvation' is redeeming the earth from the conditions that impoverish and prematurely kill millions of people, or deprive them of a life worth living, and the restoration of our beautiful planet have taken centre stage, and I feel most closely connected with the Source of all when working towards these ends.

Verses from the Bible that so inspired me as a child still inspire me today. For example: that there is 'a plan for the right time – to bring everything together in Christ, both things in heaven and things on earth in him.' (Ephesians 1.10)

However, I now relate to such ideas from a new and larger interpretive framework, one which is close to the model suggested by Theologian Sallie McFague:

'God as the embodied spirit of the universe is a personal/organic model that is compatible with interpretations of both Christian faith and contemporary science, although not demanded by either. It is a way of speaking of God's relation to all matter, all creation, that "makes sense" in terms of an incarnational understanding of Christianity and an organic interpretation of postmodern science. It helps us to be whole people within our faith and within our contemporary world.'[5]

This is an understanding where somehow (and in practice I may wrestle with how!) all is included – a truly universal, even cosmic Christian Spirituality.

Diarmuid O'muchu, in his book, *Incarnation*, speaks of the Kingdom of God as 'A collaborative endeavour for empowering love and justice, fired by the radical vision of the New Reign of God... with the historical Jesus as the exemplary disciple and all others (Christians and others) called into co-discipleship in that enterprise... It is a global enterprise embracing all that is holy and sacred within the entire web of life, cosmic and planetary alike.'[6]

In this quotation and the one above from Sallie McFague, I find the lure of the Universal. This lure inspires me and most deeply correlates with my sense of global concern.

Nothing has been lost but rather integrated into a

knowing and empowerment that comes from unexpected people and places! So where am I now? I am nowhere, which is, as I have come to see, NOW HERE!

Jane

I have always believed in God. As a child, I attended the local Methodist church with my mother and sister. I remember when I was about thirteen, feeling an inner draw to commit myself to God entirely. I considered becoming a nun as that was the only way I knew, but it didn't feel right. My belief was dormant through university, my first marriage and my first jobs. I wasn't attending a church, but like so many in the 60s and early 70s, I was interested in personal development and in new ways of thinking. Having trained as a teacher (my degree was in geology) I moved on to youth work and counselling, which I found fascinating and fulfilling. But then that inner urge for something more broke through.

As personal development had not been the answer, I reckoned it must be God. But I didn't want what I had experienced before of an hour on Sunday and not much substance through the week. I wanted something that was 24/7. So, I dropped out and started searching. I was interested in alternative health and diet as well, and became macrobiotic and rather thin. Then I read a book about a New Age spiritual community. I was so excited to discover that it was in Scotland and not in America, so in 1977 I joined the Findhorn Foundation and worked in the

Cluny kitchen for nine months. I loved my time at Findhorn. I loved all the new ideas and living in community with others of like mind. But something was still missing for me. Physically and spiritually, I still felt empty inside.

In January 1978, I had to return home. My mother had cancer of the jawbone and faced a major operation and recovery period. I sought spiritual groups in my area whilst looking after her. Then an invitation to a mission evening run by a local Pentecostal church came through our door and my mother asked me to take her. It was the first time she had left the house apart from medical appointments. It was so different from Findhorn and all the beautiful 'spiritual' people I knew. There were few there, no-one shone with an inner light, the pastor had a facial twitch, and I didn't feel at home. In response to the question 'Who wants to admit that they have been walking away from Jesus all of their life and now want to turn around and walk towards him?' my mother put up her hand while holding a tissue to her dribbling mouth with the other. I was amazed. She had been a faithful churchgoer all her life and I didn't realise there was more but she must have done. Then the twitchy pastor said to me, 'And what about you'? I said, 'Oh I'm alright, I worship with The Emissaries of Divine Light.' The look he gave me unsettled me for months.

I had become friendly with Ken and Verity who were Findhorn Foundation followers and great thinkers. Then they became Christians, so we had many debates. They invited me to a production of *The Witness* at the Royal Albert Hall and my mother and I were up in the gods. When the appeal to follow Jesus was made at the end, I stood up reluctantly. I hadn't enjoyed the musical, but I knew this was my way forward with God. Over the next few weeks, I felt an inner peace for the first time but my mind whirled with a hundred questions and uncertainties. I remember thinking that it was like going to a new country where I had to start again and learn a different language about the things of God. I talked to God about all the things I believed that were not taught now and wondered why they had to go as I could see nothing wrong with them. The answer was that they were like the walls, windows and fireplace of a house, but I was starting again with a new foundation.

I moved in with Ken and Verity and joined their charismatic Anglican church. After returning from a trip to Israel, I found all my bags packed. Verity said, 'We felt from God that you were meant to be living at home so we have told your mother and packed your bags, but you can have a cup of tea before you go!' Back in Ruislip, I went to the Anglican church at the end of the road where, after a few months, I met someone who was part of a small midweek group that started after 'Life in the Spirit' seminars.' At last, something local and exciting, so I joined the group. A couple of us went to a seminar in London about house churches as we thought they might have wisdom to share for a small Christian group. The speaker, Roger, had come over from California to start house churches here, believing that the small groups give more people a role for exercising ministry. We invited him to our group and invited others to it who had never been before. There were about fifteen of us instead of the usual handful and most came saying, 'But I don't believe in house churches.' Malcolm was there, a disillusioned missionary who had not been going to church or to our group. He invited Roger to share his vision and then said, 'How many people here think we are meant to start a house church?' There were goose bumps as every hand in the room went up, although not all felt they could attend. We started small, in our living room, with Roger and Malcolm as pastors.

I had not been working while looking after my mum and now I was wondering what to do. There was a bible college ten minutes away. I eventually decided to attend there, and started a year after I had become a committed Christian. They were exciting times as we debated biblical principles in our house church and deciding what we felt a church should be as we did not have to follow any previous tradition, so the two reinforced each other. I was part of the leadership team, so was involved in decision making and in taking services. The church grew and eventually had several small groups plus large Sunday gatherings with over a hundred people. During this period my mum died, and I later married Bill in 1990. We had a daughter, Joy, and then we adopted Grace from China.

I loved the church and all that happened as part of it. To me, God was the most important thing closely followed by church. And then that unsettling happened again. The church divided and the group we were part of built church around a soup kitchen and ministry to the poor. It moved us away from aiming for perfection to dealing with difficult situations and people, from judging and mentally excluding to acceptance – seeing Jesus in everyone. But the basic roots of an evangelical outlook were still there and for the first time it began to no longer feel like home. I could not imagine leaving as I had been involved in building this church from the beginning, but I had a dream that encouraged me to go.

We settled in an Anglican church, not evangelical, or high, or liberal, just very creative and inclusive. I remember the first Sunday there, hearing them quote a bible verse and tightening inside against the evangelical explanation I had been used to, but it did not come. I felt I could breathe again. But it was as if everything I had previously been taught and believed had turned to mush inside my head, only God remained, and it was very painful. I told God this and He said, 'You mean like inside a chrysalis?' So, the hope of it turning into a butterfly led me through. I could not read the bible every day as I used to as I could only see the old explanations, but God happily told me not to (my old pastors would not believe me). The main thing my previous church had given me that I did not lose was a love, a passion, for God.

As I recovered, I became a lay part of the leadership team. God enlarged my theology and this time it did not stop at the bounds of traditional Christianity. My first foray outside was going to a William Bloom talk on endorphins. I was so nervous as this was a bit new age like my background before I became a committed Christian. My first church had warned me against this. But it blessed me. And I remembered – I had started again with a new foundation, but I never had put back the walls, windows and fireplace. This was a very creative time, exploring spirituality in its widest sense through books and events, plus re-imagining the whole way I had looked at Christianity, led by our vicar, Rob, who turned everything inside out while making it more real. I wrote a lot, finding ways to engage with God outside the usual boxes, especially inspired by the natural world. I had three books published.

I might still be there, but Rob left and our new vicar is 'an open evangelical.' I find the teaching too simplistic, taking me back to somewhere I left long ago. For six months, I prayed and studied before each planning meeting, to bring to it what I felt represented what we had embodied previously. Then suddenly, I felt completely released. I stopped all my roles there (apart from bringing lunch once a month) and said I was retiring. That wasn't untrue, but I really felt God was leading me forward again. For the first time, I didn't feel the need to find a church that would fulfil my spiritual needs, although I do appreciate the relationships I have built up there when I go once a month.

I realised that I had been leading worship for 36 years, which felt like a significant number. I was reading about angels at the time, so I sat and talked to the angel of Christianity. I thanked him for calling me and for his graciousness, generosity and love in working with me, and then I thanked him for releasing me. He came forward and blessed me, asking me to hold out my hands. In my right palm, he put a lit white candle as the light of justice, and in my left a ceramic heart as the heart of love. Then he tied a thin, red braid around my left wrist. I found that particularly powerful as I could never have imagined it. I feel it is a symbol of his ongoing love and protection.

In my early days as a Christian, my relationship with Jesus was central. Then as my theology expanded, my focus shifted to God. I wanted to move away from addressing God as 'Lord' and sometimes used 'Oneness' or just 'Dad.' There is no word that sums up the immensity of love and 'beingness' of the divine, and I don't worry about finding the right name as I used to. I have shifted from seeing God as out there to knowing we are one, and from bothering about my failures and 'sins' to realising that God isn't bothering about them, that God does not cut us off because of 'sin;' we are all loved completely just as we are now. At the same time, I find it much easier to let go of patterns and thought forms that have been cracked and found wanting. Recently I have had a sense of the presence of Jesus again, but different from before. Originally, he was as I imagine him when on earth, intimate and loving, and wearing a wedding ring. Now I see him as a powerful heavenly being.

I want to be part of the birthing of a universal spirituality, which is the heart of what I feel Jesus came to establish but it has been packaged and controlled and eroded. I find a monthly full moon meditation to develop a group consciousness towards a universal spirituality very important and powerful. I am fed by reading books and Richard Rohr's daily meditation, by attending events, by being part of CANA so I can meet up with others on a similar path, and just by the lessons life brings. I have been particularly moved and informed by the many powerful stories of Near-Death Experiences I have heard. Bill and I meditate together every morning, and I still lead a fortnightly group called 'Godspace,' which is a rich source of relationships and support, and where we also discuss bible passages and Christian topics. I have been moved on so much, and probably will continue to be. I don't know where to, but I know that my I AM, my inner aspect of God, knows and will lead me. But at heart it is all the same. It is about God, about people, about the rich life we share with this planet, and about love.

A follower of God

To be a follower of God isn't to exchange a life of sin
for a life of safety.

It is to know the fire that birthed the universe,
to be transformed from an image breaker to an image
maker,
co-creating with God.

It isn't to celebrate history and ritual

but to dance so hard with a celebration of life
that it stamps upon injustice
and calls out the celebrant in others.

To be a follower of God
is not to build walls around a belief group
but to be part of the community of creation.

It isn't to expect beds of roses without thorns
but to know that beds of thorns will have roses.

It is a prophetic call to see and hear,
to respond with compassion and not fear anger.

It is to change the world by changing my life.

It is to be the face of God in my time.

Jane Upchurch. *Inner Wellies: Creative Space for Soul Searchers*. Christian Education. 2010.

Voices of Awakening

A particular awakening to universal truths from many traditions can be found in the following biographies.

'To become a universal human is to evolve consciously, choosing a path of development that has never been mapped before in a world that has never existed before.'[1]

Janice

There was a time, during the early nineteen-seventies, when a rapid succession of inner experiences triggered what I now see as a spiritual awakening. It was as though a curtain was being drawn back on my then immediate reality, and I could see within and beyond the limitations that my conditioned ego had hitherto set. A combination of an Anglican Church and home, a Roman Catholic convent education, and my own desire to be of service, had produced a committed Christian of ecumenical and moderately evangelical kind.

I think it was a sense of being drawn to join a weekly Meditation Group in the next town that provided the trigger for this awakening, a process that seems to have gone on ever since. I'll describe four of the experiences that were particularly life-changing and shifted my traditional exoteric understanding of Christianity to an esoteric or more inner understanding that has caused me to move beyond conventional religious adherence to a more mystical path. This path does not seem to find expression in contemporary Christianity, yet it echoes the insights of early Celtic mystics and continually affirms the depth and truth in the teachings of Jesus before these were framed into 'beliefs' by the early church fathers and many theologians ever since.

The first experience happened at the top of our own garden. I was sitting meditating, away from our children playing, when a first 'curtain' was suddenly pulled aside as it were, and I saw the amazing dance of creation and knew the oneness of all life. I experienced the cosmos not as a mechanism of some kind but as a living, sacred whole. I could see and feel a wonderfully vibrant energy flowing through everything and manifesting as the shrubs, as the insects, and as me. I felt this energy as entirely loving and beneficent and knew that everything is whole, holy – part of 'one stupendous whole whose body nature is and God the Soul,' and that if only we could 'open the immortal eye of man inwards,' we too would see the 'world in a grain of sand and heaven in a flower' as Pope and Blake have respectively expressed it.[2] I have never knowingly swatted a wasp since that day!

A second experience was, again, during a time of prayer when the inner presence I had known as the Master Jesus started speaking within my own thinking as the 'I am,' which I now realise as the Cosmic Christ. My form of communication came best through writing, and I wrote out the simple, yet profound teachings, and produced a booklet which I showed the curate at our local Church. He reacted in alarm and prayed over me, clearly assuming I was now at best 'off the wall' and at worst under the influence of the 'devil.' Reassurance came in the form of a book from the Findhorn Foundation, Eileen Caddy's *God spoke to Me.* The messages were so similar and seemed to me to echo those in the gnostic gospels and to be lived out in the Findhorn Community who were, and still are, living in a way reaching for the kingdom of heaven – as best they can and living it out on earth.

Finding no kinship in my local Church, I sought out others with whom I could share this new and deeper reality. One in particular, Ursula Burton, became a close friend. We shared our journeys which, until that point, had all been very lonely. We lived 400 miles apart, but as we explored together, each new insight seemed to come upon us at the same time. I recall the way in which we came to know that we had each of us lived many lives before this one. I seemed to go through a series of flashbacks to other times and even find places in this life that I recognised from an earlier time. Affirmation can come in strange ways if we hold fast to the 'truth' as it arises from deep within us. Then one day as we sat at breakfast together, we both saw with an inner eye a book come and land on the table amongst the toast and we knew we had to write a book together.

This book took many years in the writing, but was eventually published in 1984 as *Christian Evolution: moving towards a Global Spirituality* (Turnstone Books). Strange how, more than thirty years later, I am writing of the global spirituality emerging now as we had seen it then. At the time of publication, Ursula was leading Ignatian retreats at a Catholic Centre and was convinced she would be asked to leave. But the book seemed to strike a chord with many people, and all was well. Indeed, we received several letters, saying, 'I wept with relief when I read your book, at last appreciating that I was not alone and wasn't going mad after all.'

A third experience was during the confirmation of one of our daughters when my father (whom I knew was ill at my sister's house two hundred miles away) suddenly stood in front of me, clearly recognisable. I was overwhelmed with a huge sense of joy and realised that he must have died, and when we got home my sister rang and said that this had happened. For several days I seemed to share a totally other dimension with him, and we had some amazing conversations. I learnt how he felt I had sort of let him down by my unwillingness to discuss the possibility of his dying, which he would have found helpful. I also learnt the meaning of unconditional love. I now find that the conventional funeral service unacceptably falls short of the joy I find in the continuity of consciousness and communication that is possible with those who have transitioned to other realms.

Ursula died in 1993, but we knew that we would write another book together when she was 'on the other side.' Following her first contact with me only three hours after she had died, we started writing together in 1995. I went to Iona, a place we have both loved where the veils between the dimensions are thinner than elsewhere, and we worked together in much the way we had before only this was more of a mind-to-mind conversation and, at times, flowed like a 'mind meld.' This was easier than when we had both been in the same dimension. It has taken many years in a busy life to find time to write up all our conversations, but this book has now been published, at a time when many more of us seem ready to understand the continuity of consciousness in which birth and death are but an episode in the ongoing journey of the Soul. See (*Awakening to a New Reality: Conscious Conversations across the Horizon of Death* by Janice Dolley with Ursula Burton. Sleepy Lion Publishing, 2020.)

The Church also seems to shrink from the joy of birth and baptism, so we have asked priests to conduct Christenings for our grandchildren at home, which they have done in such uplifting ways. Truly, 'In my father's house there are many mansions.' Other dimensions of being that interpenetrate our lives can be accessible to us if we can leave behind all fear and attune with higher frequencies of being.

During this time of rapid awakening, I read avidly and attended as many conferences as I could. Sir George Trevelyan, who started the Wrekin Trust, was a particular inspiration. He spoke so insightfully of the deeper truths hidden within poetry, Shakespeare and the esoteric teachings of different faiths. Several times I visited the Findhorn Foundation, which seemed to me an example of living out the essence of Christianity. This Foundation, of which I became a trustee for fifteen years, has set out to discover and demonstrate a new vision of the Divine potential within each of us, and how we might work together in new ways, learn to trust the process of synchronicity, as Jung termed it, and seek what it really means to bring the kingdom of heaven on earth in a practical way. A key aspect of this community has been listening inwardly to 'God within' and having the sanctuary at the heart of community life. I experienced the reality of the teachings of Christ, 'Ask and you shall receive; knock and it will be opened unto you' and discovered how people of so many different backgrounds were working with the same inner realities as myself.

Nevertheless, I still thought of Jesus Christ as the way, somehow better than 'other ways.' Then I went to India. This was a fourth transforming experience, and I knew my spirituality could never be the same again. In India, spirit seems to dance more visibly through all creation, and the inner aspects of life are what life itself is really about. I remember clearly the moment when I felt that at last I was experiencing a side of my own humanity that growing up and living in the west had not given me. Here the focus is on the outer side of life, whereas in India it seems easier to connect with inner levels of being. I was travelling with one of our daughters and we visited Ashrams of different traditions. One of these was Shantivanum in the south, where we were privileged to sit with Fr. Bede Griffiths for an hour and explore the contribution of different faiths to the whole and how a 'marriage of east and west' was the way towards the emergence of a global spirituality. I returned from that first trip and engaged more actively with the growing Inter-faith Movement. In a personal way I have been drawn to the riches of the Hindu tradition and the Sufi way, but have also been enriched by meeting people and engaging in exchange with many other ways.

Nevertheless, by my second trip to India, I was still clinging to the fact that Jesus Christ was in some way more divine than the other teachers. Then came what felt like a thunderbolt from the heavens. Following exchanges at an Ashram in the Himalayas, where I was staying with our other three daughters, I was struggling with this inner tension when a huge ball of light appeared to roll down the mountain and stop at my feet. It was shaped like a tetrahedron with many, many facets. A bright light from within shone through many faces. I could see Jesus, Mohammed, Confucius, Swami Shyam (the Guru on this Ashram) and many others. From within the light a voice came clearly 'I shine through many, many teachers' and I knew that the 'I am' was too cosmically vast to be contained within any one 'son' or 'daughter' of God. Ralph Waldo Trine obviously saw this well before I did!

Let there be many windows to your soul,
That all the glory of the universe

May beautify it. Not the narrow pane
Of one poor creed can catch the radiant rays
That shine from countless sources. Tear away
The blinds of superstition; let the light
Pour through fair windows broad as Truth itself
And high as God.

     Why should the spirit peer
Through some priest-curtained orifice, and grope
Along dim corridors of doubt, when all
The splendour from unfathomed seas of space
Might bathe it with the golden waves of Love?
Sweep up the debris of decaying faiths;
Sweep down the cobwebs of worn-out beliefs,
And throw your soul wide open to the light
Of Reason and of Knowledge. Tune your ear
To all the wordless music of the stars
And to the voice of Nature, and your heart
Shall turn to truth and goodness, as the plant
Turns to the sun. A thousand unseen hands
Reach down to help you to their peace-crowned heights,
And all the forces of the firmament
Shall fortify your strength. Be not afraid
To thrust aside half-truths and grasp the whole.[3]

Poems of Passion by Ella Wheeler

In a sixteenth century insight, Shakespeare's Polonius said, 'There is more in heaven and earth, my good Horatio, than is dreamed of in your philosophy.'[4] How much more has the world moved on with quantum physics, neuroscience, and research into near death experiences, etc. Yet, outside the Church, the rational materialistic view prevails, and inside the Church, as an institution, is slowly dropping its resistance to change. To me, transformational change is an integral part of evolutionary process. I respect the Church for holding to the faith through dark and difficult ages, but its challenge today seems to be to no longer avoid the transformational process that would enable Christ's values and vision to stand against 'Mammon's' and bring heaven onto earth in the way we pray that this might happen.

The miracle that took place in Cana was the transforming of the water of the old consciousness into the wine of the new. Maybe the small organisation, CANA, who have fully supported the production of this book, is now being asked to be one of a growing number of agents of this transformation? Might the 'new wine' be the discovery of the love of the Source Of All deep within ourselves? Might the release of this love through so many be what was meant by the second coming? Might it be, as Alice Bailey put it a hundred years ago, that it is 'humanity who is now to be the world saviour?' These are amongst the questions I feel drawn to explore.

It is now in small groups that I find others with whom to explore the big questions, and in international conferences that I find a growing will to both nourish all our souls, especially those of the young who are so drowning in materiality that they often seek solace in depression or drugs. I find a longing to respect and care for the soil drenched in chemicals, the air poisoned with our fumes, the seas loaded with our pollutants. I find the Prince of Wales (Now King Charles) more often a spokesperson for the Way than either the Synod or the Vatican. Recently he quoted the late twentieth century poet, Kathleen Raine, who died in 2003: 'We are being used by invisible powers – angelic I hope – in order to bring about the changes without which this poor, beautiful earth will die, not only Nature but the soul of the world.'[5]

I respect that many friends still feel committed to work within the institutional Church. They, in turn, respect that I just cannot. It's as though I were someone in an earlier century knowing that the earth was round because I'd sailed around it and therefore unable to relate comfortably to those who continued insisting that it was flat.

As Lindsay Clarke says, 'I woke to the exhilarating sense that the unfolding flow of life was not only larger but richer in meaning and interest than my tightly managed model of it had been. I was learning to think with the heart.'[6] (*Imagining Otherwise*, a lecture published by Green Spirit Press, pamphlet no. 6)

I can no longer look backwards at an historical Christianity but feel called instead to listen to the summons of Christ now, in present time. Instead of joining my local Church community, I feel called to be part of the many communities and small groups that have started worldwide in the last few decades and are now linking up. Today, the internet spreads news of peace gatherings and vigils within hours and the new technologies are enabling people to link up across the world and share our common humanity and aspirations for a new era.

Part of my own work has been to write, with others, *The Quest: Exploring a Sense of Soul* as a framework within which people can explore their own authentic growing sense of soul. Another part has been with the Wrekin Trust and the embryonic University for Spirit and more recently with the Unity Community, which is honouring both unity and diversity, and seeking to help empower the emergence of our conscious evolution which involves collaborating to create a 'field' in which spirituality can be seen as an essential and normal aspect of life.

It seems that events are now 'soul-sized.' My prayer is that we can let go of our small concerns that divide, and instead 'Be still and know that I am God.' In this way, we can develop our sensitivity, awareness and perceptive understanding of subtle dimensions and learn to work in harmony with the higher laws of life and play our part in a great awakening in our time.

This awakening is underway. I have been discovering that leading edge science and ancient spiritual wisdom are now converging to complement personal direct experience. In combination, they affirm a whole world view that has expanded my sense of an interconnected and meaningful cosmos in which each of us has a vital part to play. Each day I seem to experience a growing sense of the oneness of all life that I had first perceived in that experience in the garden that I described earlier. The kind of love that Jesus taught and embodied seems to me to be increasingly underpinning the rich diversity of existence that many have felt is now exploding and precipitating a major cultural change as well as a widespread spiritual awakening. I find that this awakening is not only leading us towards a radical shift in how we perceive the world, but is also prompting each of us to engage more fully in the journey of transformation. I am also discovering that this inner journey is shifting many more of us from living from the level of our personalities to staying centred in the higher awareness of our deeper selves, or souls.

Finding the courage to make this shift seems to be no longer an individual option, but a collective imperative for humanity. As I meet with others, face to face or via the new zoom technologies, it seems that as a species, this shift is not only ensuring our ongoing survival but is also moving us towards fulfilling more of our evolutionary potential. It was with great delight that I discovered the work of Barbara Marx Hubbard. She was amongst the first to express the possibility that our present journey is towards developing as 'universal humans.' She wrote and spoke of the emergence of 'Homo Universalis' as our next evolutionary step. This is leading us to embody both the richness of our diversity and also the essential unity of all life. I find that a more universal expression of spirituality is spreading across all continents, which is bringing an inspiring sense of hope that, with so many more people discovering our fundamental interconnectedness, we will be able to act as a global community to protect the natural world and find ways to ensure that the needs of all are met.

Increasingly I find that this journey is no longer about 'me' but it is also about 'we' and 'all of us together.' It is from Africa that we have been given the phrase of Ubuntu. 'I am because you are.' It seems that day by day I am learning to expand my compassion more widely. Each day I experience a little more of what it is to live fully in the present moment, learning from the past but trusting that each next step will be shown, even during difficult times.

This 'sutra,' as he calls it, came through a friend who is on a similar track as myself and expresses this idea better than I am able:

'Fools walk backwards into the future
Thinking that the past
Is leading them somewhere
The wise leave the path behind
In the eternal now
They step into the abyss
Knowing that the Way
Will form beneath their feet.'

We have inherited a world that is based on what our

predecessors thought and created. Now it is up to us, all of us I think, to discover and undertake the part that we are asked to play in building a new era we may well find is a fulfilment of all that Jesus taught and demonstrated. After each healing, did he not say, 'Go and do likewise'?

Don

Beginnings are important in anyone's spiritual journey, and mine were in the Midlands. I was born in Birmingham in 1952 and moved to Leicester at the age of six. My parents were fairly regular church-goers, and as such I went to a Presbyterian Sunday School until the age of nine, when the chance of swimming on a Sunday morning presented itself as a much more attractive option than sitting on the splintering floor of a cold church hall.

I had a very secure upbringing in a middle-class family, which resulted in me emerging as a fairly self-contained, rather shy individual in my teens. I went successfully through the state education system, which taught me (or encouraged in me) logical, critical, rational thinking. I was good at the sciences and maths and always interested in how things work. I wanted to know why the world was as it was. In my late teens, I could probably be categorised as agnostic, seeing the universe as a physical unit functioning according to the laws of cause and effect. There were still questions rumbling around, however, like 'What is at the end of the universe?' 'How did it all start?' 'Is there other life out there?'

'What about other dimensions?' and 'What about ghosts, UFOs, and other paranormal, supernatural events?' I discovered the science fiction genre just at the dawn of its explosion into the area of science fantasy. I read and read, picking up ideas and possibilities that fed my philosophically questing brain; I read all about the idea of other dimensions or states of being. The possibility of sentient forces or a god or gods became real.

In 1975, after I finished at University, Jayne and I married, and in 1978 I started teaching science in a local comprehensive school in Leicester. During the next few years, we started to question the meaning of our lives and our way of life. We became involved in ecological issues and the 'alternative' movement and began to look into the existence of a spiritual dimension to life.

As time progressed, I started to break out of the rational, western, scientific mode of thinking, and became a seeker for meaning and experience in life. I was very interested in the supernatural, and in ecology. I felt there must be a better way of living than the model offered by the British culture of the late seventies. I was looking for a harmonious way of life, a way of being where community and people were important, with meaning to life, something to work towards, to give direction. We both became active in the Ecology Party (now the Green Party), and visited a number of communities and people trying to live a simpler, ecologically-sound lifestyle in Britain.

At some stage in this, I read a book called *The Secret Life of Plants* by Christopher Tompkins and Peter Bird, which documented the experiments done to show that plants had a form of consciousness and responded to emotions. You may remember when you were encouraged to love your plants and talk to them. For me, it connected the natural world and environment with the world of thought, mind and emotion in a scientific way. This led me to reading about the Findhorn Community in Scotland, where enormous vegetables had been grown through following the advice of 'plant spirits,' or 'devas' and 'God' speaking to members of the community. It was exciting, stimulating stuff, as it made a further connection for me between the paranormal and the spiritual.

During this time, Jayne experienced a period of mental and emotional illness, which she had suffered from since childhood, and through that illness I reached the end of my 'self,' my own resources, and started to really reach out to God. I had tried everything I knew to help, along both the medical path and a range of complementary therapies, all to no avail. In this situation of desperation, I cried out from my depths, "If there is a God, help!" That was the awakening of my spirit. This led me to looking into such things as tree and plant spirits, pyramid power, alternative medicine, pendulum dowsing and divining, ley lines and centres of spiritual power, and the spirit within. It was the last of those that became more important for me as time went on. The world within and its connection with the spiritual fascinated me.

Jayne and I eventually met an elderly woman and her daughter who 'channelled,' or got in touch with those they called the 'Masters.' These Masters told them about the 'Ancient Wisdom' that lies behind all of life, physical and spiritual. (The woman had three large filing cabinets full of audio tapes of the Masters speaking through them!) The Ancient Wisdom contained the secrets of life, how to progress spiritually to eventually achieve oneness with the Ultimate Being. Part of that path was to attain Christ-Consciousness. They put me in touch with other writings I sent off for and tried to follow. I became interested in Helena Blavatsky and Theosophy, and read a lot of Alice Bailey's writings, which were a mixture of eastern esotericism, Theosophy, and Christianity. For a couple of years, I meditated daily using the 'Great Invocation' and called down the White Light, trying to reach higher levels of awareness, of Christ-consciousness.

As my reading and seeking continued, I came to a belief in God (as the Ultimate Being), in prayer, and in Jesus the Christ, as an ordinary person who attained the full measure of 'Christ-consciousness,' the first to do so, not as Saviour or Son of God. Accordingly, I became more interested in who Jesus actually was. A series of events led to my wife and me attending a church in Leicester on Easter Sunday 1983, where we were very moved by the love, openness and life that we saw emanating from the people there. At the same time, I was puzzled by the life of Jesus and the meaning of the cross. I thought I had access to knowledge beyond

Christianity to deeper, timeless truths, but what I saw was a friendly, warm, living, loving community that embodied more experientially the truths I had been seeking in 'The Ancient Wisdom,' and it all seemed to revolve around this man Jesus and his death and resurrection.

I turned to Christianity aged 30, through a combination of thinking, reading, asking questions and the influence of that loving church. Whilst on holiday in Pembrokeshire in the summer of 1983, I had a profound conversion experience of God's love and my heart was opened, and because of our attendance at that loving church and its framework of teaching, my path became that of a 'born-again' charismatic evangelical Christian. During the following seven years, I prayed in tongues, practised deliverance ministry, had a curse cast out of me, and had numerous profound experiences of what was termed 'baptism in the Holy Spirit', but what I would now prefer to call an experience of oneness with the divine or unitive consciousness. I always knew, somewhere in my 'knower,' that my previous experience in and understanding of the New Age sphere was not wasted.

In 1989, I began to feel the call to ordination and priesthood in the Anglican Church. I gradually went through the selection process and ended up in 1991 going to St. Johns College in Nottingham. During the theological training course, I explored all my New Age experience in a dissertation entitled *The New Age Critique of the Church – what can we learn from it?* It showed me that I was still very interested in what is now known as contemporary or holistic spirituality and I also discovered much more about the whole breadth of spirituality within the Christian Church, especially the mystical tradition.

In 1993 we moved to Sutton Coldfield, where I was a curate in a large evangelical church, a very busy place. The following year, my sister was diagnosed with an aggressive cancer and Jayne became pregnant with our third child and started displaying signs of depression and panic attacks. In rapid succession, our first and much-loved dog died, then my sister died, our third daughter was born two weeks later, and Jayne was admitted to hospital the next week, remaining there for two months with severe post-natal suicidal depression. We came through it eventually. I survived by coping and shutting down to any threatening emotions. Two years later, I decided to have some secular counselling to unpack my own feelings around that time, which I had clamped down.

In 1996, we moved back to Leicester, for me to be a team vicar in a small suburban church, which was a huge contrast from the curacy and my previous parish experience, although a similar area to where I had taught for years. Three years later, I accepted the post of chaplain at Loughborough University. It was there that I became the New Religious Movement's Advisor for the Diocese of Leicester and started looking into the whole area of contemporary spirituality again. I joined CANA and was relieved to find a group of people who were thinking along the same lines as I was, which is that Christianity has to be freed from the shackles of the medieval mindset and get back to the original inspiration of the Christ.

I then moved to Pembrokeshire as vicar of several rural churches with very traditional viewpoints. I was still within the Christian tradition, but operating from a much wiser place. In 2017, after 24 years of church ministry, I retired. During all this time, I have been interested in various areas of spirituality, but found it desperately hard at times to make the time to do any serious reading. I have very much appreciated the wisdom of spiritual direction and become familiar with techniques of counselling and psychotherapy. I have dabbled in creation spirituality, Gnosticism and mysticism, and Celtic spirituality, and I have enjoyed the insights of techniques such as the Myers-Briggs Personality Inventory and the Enneagram. I have been drawn to the silence of contemplative prayer and meditation, the wisdom of the mystics, and more liberal and radical theology. Moreover, I have been walking joyfully into a deeper understanding of the spiritual path, reading all sorts of other teachings outside of the church, ranging from quantum physics to metaphysics and the spiritual realms, and perceiving many connections between the two. I have increasingly felt that I want to find, or develop, a spirituality that can give a frame of reference for understanding the world as it is, particularly drawing on the Perennial Wisdom or Esoteric Philosophy tradition. There seems to be emerging a path towards a more universal spirituality that respects and honours the traditions of the past but seeks to move on into the future with a new understanding of those traditions.

I respect and hold dear the traditions and theology of two thousand years, but also see that to reach a new generation, the theology of the church has to evolve to a new place, a new world. This is one of the problems we have when we come to reading the bible or church doctrine and the creeds – we inhabit a totally different world view from the biblical times. Heaven is not up, it is not part of this physical universe. Hell is not beneath us. The second coming is not going to happen with Christ literally riding in on clouds of glory. We have moved on in our understanding of the nature of the world. In biblical times, mental illness was thought to be caused by evil spirits. Medical treatment then was basic, with no anaesthetics or antibiotics, sewage systems were primitive, and justice systems were brutal. We no longer stay with biblical or medieval thought about everything else – medicine, science, politics, social structure – but for some reason many people think they have to stay with medieval theology that developed in an entirely different world view. To my mind, we have to interpret Christianity through 21st century spectacles. In 2012 I had a book published, which started to do some of that, linking up some of the new scientific insights from quantum physics and epigenetics to go beyond traditional theological interpretations of the Christ event and link with the idea of global shift that is now happening, as human consciousness moves up a gear to a new place. I called it *Blue Sky God: the Evolution of Science and Christianity*. As I've said, we live in a different world and I now stand with one foot in the Christian tradition and the other firmly engaged carving a path towards a more universal spirituality, drawing on the Ageless Wisdom teachings, and a much bigger cosmology than the bible presents us with. I'm hoping to write more along those lines in years to come, and I'm happy where I now stand, as an open-minded, open-hearted, holistic follower of the Jesus teachings, seeking to raise my own level of consciousness and contribute my part to the raising of humanity's.

Linking Piece

And so, we come to the end our biographies; we will see many of their themes reflected in the remaining chapters. Taken together, they provide a rich tapestry of many vicissitudes, facets and journeys of faith, lived with integrity.

We have found that many people have not felt nourished within their local parishes and find an increasing difference between the official teachings of the church and how they experience their faith on a daily basis. We recognise that many changes are taking place within the church and within the evolving lay movements growing up within and alongside Christianity. However, large established institutions, like the church, find it difficult to change at the pace necessary and are sometimes subject to vested interests that slow down or try to prevent change.

Writing in the 1980s, Jesuit priest Hugo Enomiya-Lassalle suggested that religion needed to reorient itself in the light of evolutionary changes in humankind, otherwise it would not survive.

Catholic theologian Karl Rahner suggested, 'The Christian of the future will be a mystic or he or she will not exist at all.'[7]

More recently, Pope Francis has advised:

'If we go in search of other people, other cultures, other ways of thinking, other religions, we come out of ourselves and begin that beautiful adventure that is called "dialogue." Dialogue is very important for one's maturity, because in relation with other people, relations with other cultures, also in healthy relations with other religions, one grows; grows, matures.'[8]

The thrust for this change is impelling us forward from within. The choice we have is to move with it or hold fast until the old paradigms change and in some cases inevitably crumble. New horizons call us to journey forward.

The winds of change are blowing through all established institutions, including the church. The institutional church has so much to offer a needy world. It is as the institutional church embraces more fully some of the changing dynamic that is under way, illustrated in the biographies, that it will be able to nourish its own members and continue as source of love, healing and reconciliation in the world.

PART THREE

Towards a Universal Understanding

Chapter 1: Towards the Universal Within Western Christianity

We talk of 'Universal Spirituality.' Not wanting to create yet another religion, I see universal spirituality as the binding force that brings us all together with a strong desire for justice, peace, care for others and endeavour to rescue the planet from destruction. Individuals and groups outside any religious persuasion as well as those within specific religious organisations may be party to this in whatever way that allows the freedom to express love and acceptance for all that is. CELIA

Religion is not independent of culture; it is both shaped by and informs the surrounding society. Religious traditions 'bear the imprint of a particular society and culture. There can come a time when these methods, these outward forms, no longer answer the deepest needs of humanity.'[1] (Cyprian Smith, *The Way of Paradox*)

Now, as we face so much change and upheaval globally, it unsurprisingly impacts on religious adherence and beliefs.

Christianity, currently regarded as the largest world religion in general, although predicted to be eclipsed by Islam in the coming decades, is of course feeling, or sometimes barricading from, these winds of change. Perhaps less acknowledged is the interrelationship between an individual's spirituality and surrounding culture, particularly as many who would consider themselves spiritual but not religious have to some extent rejected institutional religion and are carving a more independent path to new deeper meaning and way of living. However, as it has been generally recognised, no person is an island, and therefore no one can escape the influence of the cultural milieu into which they are born and live.

One of our biographers expresses her desire for a more universal understanding and relates it to the original teachings of Jesus: 'I want to be part of the birthing of a universal spirituality, which is the heart of what I feel Jesus came to establish but it has been packaged and controlled and eroded.' JANE

Change is not new, but as life becomes more complicated at an accelerated pace, this leaves many people overwhelmed and confused. Globalisation and the relative ease of travel have given rise to a greater encounter with other cultures and world views. Furthermore, the internet, social media, and telecommunication have made available knowledge previously in the province of but a few people. This encounter and exposure to other cultures and perspectives can stimulate an expanded worldview, and shifts many people of faith into a more universal perspective.

One example of this is the discovery of the practice of meditation by young people travelling to India in the later decades of the last century. It is now being more widely adopted along with other practices such as yoga, tai chi and qigong. This is causing many to seek out communities of belonging that are aligned with these practices rather than remain with those who prefer a previously proscribed practice.

Janet alludes to the need for a more universal spirituality: 'The exploration of a more universal spirituality seems vital to me if we are to meet the challenges of the day from a creative and unifying place, rather than a destructive and divisive one.'

According to Clay Shirky, a writer and theorist on Collapse from Complexity, we are seeing the faltering and even collapse of many systems and institutions. He suggests that to build a new future, people are needed who can 'Escape the complexities of the old systems and who figure out how to work simply in the present.' He asserts that they are the ones 'who get to have the most influence on the future.'[2]
https://meh.religioused.org/web/tensegrities/2010/04/02/clay-shirky-on-collapse-from-complexity/

It can be seen that for many Christians and adherents of other spiritual traditions, a new and hopeful simplicity is emerging today, especially through the rise in contemplative practices.

The heart of Christian contemplation is 'an awakening of pure consciousness, an unconditioned illumination and realization of the core of the Person, the point of a primordial oneness with God.'[3]

This simplicity emerges through growing realisation that, in essence, all are intrinsic parts of one whole, with microscopic actions, thoughts, feelings and actions feeding into and affecting the macro level. Learning to work and see from Oneness can bring about a universal element to faith and care for all life.

Janet refers to this sense of oneness: 'The mystical way I'd been introduced to in the contemplative religious community seemed to be about the idea of our oneness with all through letting go, self-emptying (kenosis), and silence.'

It is through embracing this that many Christians find themselves revitalised and reenergised to be a source of love, healing and reconciliation in the world. Indeed, in his Papal encyclical, Fratelli Tutti, Pope Francis addresses Catholics and all people of goodwill: 'The development of a global community of fraternity based on the practice of social friendship on the part of all peoples and nations calls for a better kind of politics, one truly at the service of the common good.'

In the Western world, the new developments are sometimes described in terms of evolving or emerging Christianity. They are in part a response to the need to connect beyond our local and tribal belonging and see the bigger picture.

It is important to note that there are also people who are looking back, becoming more conservative, seeing their faith as a bastion against rapid and unsettling change. Their unchanging beliefs give rise to certainty and security.

Others, to whom this book is giving voice, are ordinary people who are encountering a shift in religious understanding and lived spiritual experience. They are embracing the evolutionary nature of their faith and are finding a sense of wholeness rather than separation and a mystical approach that values the direct experience of the Divine.

It is being suggested that we may be heading for, or are already experiencing, an 'Axial shift.'

Axial Shifts

As we read through the biographies, each expressing different experiences of a change within, there seems to be emerging such a widespread departure from the 'old' that future historians may look back on these times as an axial shift. The term axial age was coined by philosopher Karl Jaspers. The first such period was when there was an evolution in human consciousness that led to the formation of our great religious traditions between roughly 800-200 BCE. Episcopal priest Rev Matthew Wright suggests 'the First Axial Age opened for us the possibility of the transcendent and a personal quest for enlightenment or salvation, it also tended to break our earlier, primal sense of collective identity (rooted in tribe) and our deep, felt connection to Earth.[4]

Second Axial Age

Some commentators have suggested that we may now be

experiencing a Second Axial age. Technological advancements that affect almost everything have transformed the way of life for most people and cultures, and this leads to people perceiving the world in new ways. Attendance and membership in traditional, institutionalised religions has declined in many industrialized nations since the mid-20th century. This shift is related closely to the process of globalization, and for many, there is an emerging sense of oneness and universality, a recognition that we are one human family, sharing one planet in crisis, one intricately interwoven tapestry of life.

For many who remain within the church or exist at the margins, the shift underway today is from a heaven-focused spirituality that had initially placed great emphasis on transcending the world and the human condition to one leading to an appreciation of the interconnectedness of all life.

Magda alludes to this, suggesting that her 'focus is on the interconnectedness of all life and deeper engagement with humanity, and an appreciation of our place within the whole cosmos.'

Pope Francis is one of the powerful voices within Christianity giving voice to a more universal concern, beautifully expressed in the following prayer.

The encyclical, Laudate Si, written by Pope Francis in 2015, was a call to the Christian world to come together in recognition of our growing awareness and our responsibility as humanity to cherish and care for all life. This is the prayer that he circulated in the same year:

> 'Oh powerful God you are present in the whole universe
> and in the smallest of your creatures
> You embrace with your tenderness all that exists
> Pour out upon us the power of your love
> that we may protect life and beauty
> Fill us with peace that we may live
> as brothers and sisters harming no one
> O God of the poor
> help us to rescue the abandoned and forgotten of this
> earth...'[5]

In subsequent chapters, we set out to articulate some of the main features of the shift occurring within Christianity, aligning people to a more universal care and concern.

Chapter 2: Influence of Science leading to an increasing Universal Awareness

In this chapter, we will examine the relationship between science, religion and spirituality. In particular, we look at how the field of science, which had become increasingly atheistic until the 20th century, is now leading many towards a more spiritual and universal perspective, thanks to relatively recent scientific discoveries.

As one of our biographers noted, 'I respect and hold dear the traditions and theology of two thousand years, but also see that to reach a new generation, the theology of the church has to evolve to a new place, a new world.' DON

The rise of science happened in an age when the prevailing thought-form was that the whole universe was alive, and God was viewed as being present within the natural world. Saint Francis is well known for his 'Canticle to Brother Sun and Sister Moon,' as well as preaching to animals, who were thought to have souls. The world was deemed to be charged with Spirit.

This view of the Cosmos began to change in the 17th Century with the rise of scientific materialism. The French philosopher Descartes, famous for postulating, 'I think therefore I am,' saw mind and heaven as separate from the material world. He developed the view that the world was mechanistic and followed its own laws. Humans to him were the sole creatures with a conscious mind. In this view, animals were seen as machine-like, acting only on instinct.

The scientific materialism that eventually developed is based on the belief that only matter exists. The Cosmos is essentially a soul-less machine, devoid of purpose and meaning as matter in the materialist conception is not conscious and humans have arrived in the universe by sheer chance. This view has profound implications for our beliefs about God and the world. It affects our mental health, our cultural development and humanity's relationship to the natural world and indeed the whole Cosmos. With the advent of materialism in science came the belief that our fundamental reality is purely physical and that all other phenomena arise from it. Consequently, religion and science drifted apart and were often seen as opposing world views, since the materialist paradigm is basically atheistic.

However, with a growing movement towards modifying or rejecting materialism, and new discoveries in many fields of science now seeming to correlate with the understanding of reality embraced by humanity's mystics, some are even suggesting that religion and science need each other. They answer different needs and questions, and rather than being in opposition to each other, they can be seen as complementary spheres of knowledge, each with a crucial contribution to make to the development and sustainability of the earth and all life.

Many of the underlying assumptions of scientific materialism are being called into question, and recent discoveries, particularly those in the realm of quantum physics, are leading to new ideas that can be interpreted as more in alignment with a faith-inspired worldview and indeed as corroborating the insights of ancient mystics.

Here is a brief introduction to some of the developments in science that are influencing change in Christian belief.

Evolutionary Theory

When Evolutionary Theory first emerged, it was rejected by many people of faith and disturbed the world view of those who had taken the creation accounts in Genesis in a very literalistic way. Yet Darwin himself did not see a dichotomy between evolution and a belief in God, and doubts he harboured for part of his life arose from the early death of his beloved daughter, Anne, from tuberculosis at the age of 10.

'It seems to me absurd to doubt that a man may be both an ardent Theist and an Evolutionist... I have never been an atheist in the sense of denying the existence of a God'.[1] Darwin in a Letter to John Fordyce.

In recent decades, an evolutionary view of life and indeed Christianity has taken greater hold, and many leading faith-based thinkers are embracing it with great vigour and seeing it as a springboard to growth and participation in continued evolutionary unfolding. One of the earliest Christian thinkers to embrace an evolutionary world view was Teilhard de Chardin who saw that 'We are the latest arrivals in an evolutionary universe; we emerge from the whole and are integral to it.'[2]

Teilhard also suggested that this evolutionary unfolding was divinely guided, leading to a future unity he called the Omega point.

Evolutionary theory can change a view of God away from that of a creator who withdrew from the world, intervening only occasionally and out of reach except through prayer and worship. The process of evolution can be viewed as suggestive of a Divine presence intimately involved in and sustaining all life as the vitality within everything. This was well expressed by Jill in her story: 'My present faith is based on reinterpreting Christianity in light of modern understanding of an evolving cosmos, of which we are an integral part. This evolution is powered and guided by an underlying creative, loving life force, which I call 'God'. Human beings are variously conscious of the cosmic life force urging us to evolve to wholeness, higher consciousness and selflessness and to become one with God.'

Quantum Physics

The field of Quantum Physics, which studies the smallest known particles, has presented us with vastly divergent data and theories from the understandings previously held. New understandings are now filtering out from the study of Quantum Physics into other fields and are causing a revision in ideas about how the world works. It's a huge field of learning, complex and challenging to understand, and yet it is creating shifts in contemporary thought.

One feature, that of quantum entanglement, has caused excitement in spiritual communities. It demonstrates that, at least at a sub-atomic level, particles can be linked across vast areas of space. No matter how far apart, changes in one particle will be instantaneously mirrored in the linked particle, and this has been proven experimentally. This is sometimes referred to as non-local action at a distance and seems to happen outside of this space-time continuum.

The other major insight from quantum physics is that in order for the wave form of a particle to become material substance, it has to be observed, which implies that a consciousness has to observe it. In turn, this implies that consciousness, or mind, has to exist before matter, which is a controversial topic and has increasing support from non-materialist scientists. This and other insights from the study of the quantum world do seem to support the idea of relational holism, which points to the interconnected nature of reality and that something or someone can be both distinct and part of the whole: unity in diversity.

The study of the subatomic levels of the universe also points to the idea that in effect everything is composed of vibrational energies, and that we are, as Don MacGregor puts it, 'all interconnected, swirling patterns of energy, and that the same patterns of information are repeated at all levels of being'.[3]

From this discovery, contemporary spiritual thinking has begun to emphasise that as 'swirling energy,' we are able to have a far greater influence on the shape of things than hitherto understood. Some would say that every thought, prayer, and action has efficacy. We therefore need to be careful not just of our actions but of our thoughts as well!

Another aspect causing pause for thought is that currently 95% of the universe is thought to be non-material or non-visible. Theories about dark matter and dark energy, thought to be present in the non-visible universe, add to the sense of mystery, and some ponder whether the non-visible also equates with spiritual realms of being. Certainly, relatively recent discoveries point towards quantum forces of energy within the universe that hold things together. These forces can be said to have qualities of attraction and surrender, and in evolution it can be said that forces of attraction and submission exist for the development of the whole, leading many to see these as further evidence that a force of love is at the heart of the universe.

The findings of modern science and understandings of mystics seem to be converging in many aspects, especially in a growing awareness of the web of connection not just on earth but throughout the universe and between material and non-material realms. Albert Einstein wrote that 'A human being is a part of the whole, called by us "Universe," a part limited in time and space.'[4]

He went on to suggest that many experience themselves as separate from everything else rather than as part of the whole as mystics and many scientists suggest. He denotes this feeling of separation as 'a kind of optical delusion of his consciousness.'

Consciousness Studies

This is a new and rapidly developing field and it presents an alternative to scientific materialism, which regards consciousness as the property of brains, primarily those of humans. Through a materialist view, the universe has no ultimate meaning and humans and animals are basically machines. However, this view gives rise to consciousness being regarded as the 'hard problem' as there is no adequate explanation for how it arises.

Now, in part due to the development of quantum physics, many are arriving at the opinion that, 'There is one consciousness of which we are each an individualised being. Consciousness itself is described as the Ground of Being, which has also been used as a Christian term for God.'[5] (Don MacGregor, *Christianity Expanding – Into Universal Spirituality.*)

A significant percentage of people now believe that there is in effect only one consciousness, of which we are all a part. In Christian tradition, as in other religious traditions, consciousness is seen as deriving from beyond the brain, arising from God or ultimate consciousness, which underlies the whole of reality. Therefore, this is another field in which the views held by post-materialist scientists and religious thought are converging.

Dr Jude Currivan provides more detailed evidence for the understanding that 'Consciousness is not something that we have but what we and the whole world are.'[6]

Some postulate that different levels of consciousness exist. For example, there are numerous books and studies that demonstrate how plants and trees have some form of consciousness and communication and can send warning signals to other members of their species in the face of threats. A fascinating book in this respect has been written by Merlin Sheldrake, called *Entangled Life: How Fungi Make Our Worlds, Change Our Minds and Shape Our Futures*.

It has been discovered that fungi form vast underground networks, sometimes referred to as the 'wood-wide web,' through which they communicate and deliver nutrients. This is transforming the way we understand the ecosystem and life on Earth. Without fungi there would be no plant life and in this and other ways human existence depends on fungi.

Consciousness is increasingly coming to be seen as fundamental to existence – that matter arises out of consciousness, rather than the other way around. Recent experimental data suggests that consciousness affects matter and that the consciousness, intentions and expectations of a researcher can change the results of an experiment.

Although not fully understood, seen in the above ways, consciousness can lead once more to the world and cosmos being experienced as a living organism whose origin is in the consciousness of God.

Cosmology

From a context of personal faith, such as within our local village or town, the context of a global village in an expanding universe emerges. For example, the Hubble and James Webb telescopes and other space exploration have made available images of a far vaster universe than had previously been visible, with trillions of stars and billions of galaxies. Whilst these discoveries of a far larger cosmos than was previously thought are exciting for some, others find themselves lost, fearful and insignificant. Several of our biographers refer to the need for carving out faith in the context of a much larger cosmology than presented in the Bible.

The growth of Cosmology is very significant in focussing our attention not just on our place within planet earth, but also within the wider universe. In recent decades, science fiction has opened our imaginations to both the vastness of the universe, the possibilities of other universes beyond our own and the potential for space travel for future generations. Looking up at the night sky can give us the insight expressed in the psalms of David who, perhaps whilst a shepherd on the hills, looked up in awe and in the light of this vastness questioned 'What is man that You are mindful of him?'[7]

In her biography, Magda refers to the need for a 'larger interpretive framework,' something many people are discovering. As cosmological discoveries reveal a much larger known universe than previously humanly apprehended, so our frame of reference expands.

These discoveries impinge on our awareness, and we begin to see things in a wider perspective than ever before. The earth is no longer seen as the physical centre of the universe, which in turn is no longer seen as static but as evolving and expanding. This can lead to the recognition that our apprehension of truth and the answers to ultimate questions might also be evolving rather than fixed, requiring an acceptance of the provisional nature of our beliefs.

Cosmology stimulates questions about the place of planet earth and of humankind within it. All the above necessitate interpreting knowledge in the light of a much bigger picture. A holistic spirituality cannot be solely about individual salvation but must take into account the salvation of humankind and indeed the future of the cosmos. Arguably this has led many awakening Christians to an emphasis on the Kingdom of God, inspiring them to work beyond the confines of the Church, believing that eventually the Kingdom of God will be brought about within the whole cosmos. Here is an example from the biographies:

'Whilst some feel anxiety and a sense of being lost and alone when considering the new understandings of the sheer magnitude of the cosmos, others find it a cause for humble exploration. However, there were still questions rumbling around such as, 'What is at the end of the universe?' 'How did it all start?' 'Is there other life out there'? 'What about other dimensions?' and 'What about ghosts, UFOs, and other paranormal, supernatural events?'

Deep Time

Current estimates put the age of the Universe at 13.7 billion years old (give or take a few million!) and the earth at 4.54 billion years old. This is way beyond the earlier estimates of a few million years during the 19th and early 20th centuries, and recognising this gives rise to the concept of deep time.

The concept of deep time is drawn from geological study. In the 18th century, geologist James Hutton suggested that Earth was a lot older than most people thought. At the time the Earth was estimated to be six million years old. Later the phrase 'deep time' was coined by John McPhee in his 1981 book, *Basin and Range*: 'Numbers do not seem to work well with regard to deep time. Any number above a couple of thousand years – fifty thousand, fifty million – will with nearly equal effect awe the imagination.'[8]

The current Anthropocene Age is characterised as the age in which humankind has had undue effect on the planetary environment, yet it is a relatively young age. For some, the awe of deep time has led to a sense of connection to a force much older, creating a need to become co-creators in the future evolution of planet and people. For others, it has caused a disruption to faith, making the Divine seem further away and unreachable, finding difficulty in conceiving that the creator/spirit of all may have been at work in creation long before the dawn of humankind.

An understanding that the world was created billions of years ago, and that humanity is a relatively late introduction, can lead to greater humility regarding our tendency to dogmatism. Reflecting on this new scale of time helps us to realise with greater humility that, after all, humanity as it is may not be the pinnacle of creation and that our beliefs can only be provisional and may need periodic readjustment.

Near Death Experiences (NDEs) and Out-of-Body Phenomena

For several decades, there has been a growth in serious scientific study into the previously little known or taboo subjects of near-death and out-of-body experiences. With advances in medicine ensuring that many people can be brought back to life from a state of near-death, a new field of study, that of near-death experiences, has grown. Scientific study into near-death experiences and peoples' experience of contact with those who have died is leading to a growing awareness of the continuation of consciousness beyond death. One such organisation is IANDS, the International Association for near-death Studies, which publishes research and offers support to people who experience

NDEs.[9]

As have so many others, Jane reports that she had 'been particularly moved and informed by the many powerful stories of near-death Experiences that I have heard.'

Countless reports of near-death experiences document a sense of people leaving their bodies and being drawn into a realm of light and indescribable beauty and love. Many also report a life review in which they see scenes from their lives, often from the perspective of the people around them. There is no sense of external judgement, more a moment of growth and understanding rather than a punitive process.

Whilst brain scans show that following clinical death there is no discernible brain activity, many people report that during this time the reality they experience appears more vivid and real than life in the body. This is borne out by research that shows that people's memory of these experiences does not fade over the years as would a dream. In fact, they often result in changed lives, as love, compassion, and relationships become more important than material success. The growing literature and data on these experiences can help us all to see our present life in a wider context than hitherto.

It can be seen that the ongoing discoveries of science need to be integrated with our understanding of the world and the development of theology and faith. The findings of post-materialist science open the possibility that all are expressions of the one consciousness and that the material world exists within a stupendous whole. Our knowledge, both scientific and beyond science, expands as new discoveries are made, so too our thinking needs to be open to review and change.

Chapter 3: Influences on Christian Thought Beyond the World of Science

Beyond the world of science, other developments in our world challenge us to form a more universal perspective. Here are a few of them.

Globalisation

'Globalization is not a monolithic force but an evolving set of consequences – so some good, some bad and some unintended, it is the new reality.'[1] (John B. Larsen)

Whilst many experience a sense of being uprooted and lost in the expanding boundaries of global trade, technological and economic development, others develop a new sense of belonging at a global and universal level, some people identifying as Global or World citizens. This wider sense of belonging can create a sense of unease if not matched by a sense of local rootedness, but one which at the same time expresses a wider more universal sense of identity.

When faced with a potential precarious future, there is a dawning realisation that we must not rely on politicians alone but engage citizens at the grassroots level, whether at the local, national and global levels, to provide the love and endeavour that will build the better world that our hearts know is now needed. Acting and relating at both global and local levels have become motivating factors for many Christians and people from other faith traditions, and a variety of secular individuals.

Another driver of change, related to global shifts and which will become increasingly important, is the mass displacement of people, caused through the evermore serious effects of climate change, oppression, and conflict. The UN estimates that in 2020 there were 82 million displaced people across the world. This exposes us to other cultures and thought forms unless we head for the bunker and wear metaphorical blinkers!

The development of Interfaith dialogue, action and inter-spirituality

Some of those who are questioning and not always finding a home within the Christian tradition suggest that there is a lure towards a more universal understanding as they meet and work with neighbours from other cultures and traditions. They then feel prompted to embrace a more expansive framework for their lives than they had encountered in Christianity as they had received and perceived it. An immensely influential figure in recent decades, Archbishop Desmond Tutu, stated, 'God is not upset that Gandhi was not a Christian, because God is not Christian! All of God's children and their different faiths help us to realize the immensity of God.'[2]

Kate writes, 'Having dipped a little into other world faiths, especially Buddhism and Hinduism, I have never accepted the Church, or Christianity, as the only path to a relationship with God.'

Many of our biographers give voice to the nurture and learning they have received from other faith traditions.

With globalisation comes pluralism and knowledge of other religions and spiritual paths, leading more people to a search for the universal truth at the heart of all the world's religions. Consciously and unconsciously, there is cross-fertilisation as ideas permeate religious boundaries, and many are finding nourishment in the teachings and practices of other faiths. One of our biographers, Celia, points out that at their group 'there were Buddhists, a Hindu and two Sufis. It made no difference.'

There is an increasing espousal of the value of faith traditions beyond Christianity, with a profound interfaith and inter-pilgrim dialogue underway. Instead of feeling threatened by the insights and practices of other faiths, many are finding themselves enriched by them, and even finding their own path within the Christian faith deepened by this sharing. Fr Basil Pennington, one of the people involved in developing the practice of Centering Prayer, suggests a way of praying that takes us beyond our own tradition. 'It answers to the deepest aspirations of all religious persons, whatever their tradition, whatever was the first experience out of which grew their particular expression of faith.'[3]

Interfaith relations are growing, not only at the local level, with groups who meet together to discover others' beliefs and practices, but also increasingly to act together for societal change, in the fields of economic justice, peace-making, and climate change. It is also taking place at a more global level.

The first worldwide calling together of religions was made by the Indian Swami Vivekananda, who held the first Parliament of World Religions in Chicago in 1893. A second centennial parliament was held in both Chicago and Bangalore in India in 1993. It has grown to be recognised as the foremost global convenor of interfaith and inter-spiritual grassroots change-makers. In 2023, it returned to its birthplace in Chicago to celebrate its 130 years of existence. It continues in its vision to bring harmony and understanding between religious and spiritual communities and foster engagement with the world, and its institutions, and looks to address the issues of the time.

The World Congress of Faiths is another long-standing interfaith body. It began in 1936 and continues as a movement welcoming individuals who share its values, bringing them together for both dialogue and action. It produces a journal, *Interreligious Insight*.

Psychological Approaches

'I was to find God in the depths rather than in the heights and there was a coming together of my psychological and spiritual searching, which I'd kept very separate until then. I came to realise they had been interweaving, creating a tapestry of what my life is about.' JANET

The above realisation by Janet is not uncommon. The need for an integration of both psychological and spiritual insights is echoed in another biography: 'Although I have been a student of the work of Carl Jung and other psychologists over the last thirty years, I don't see how psychology alone can provide all the answers.' JUDY

As the fields of psychology and psychotherapy have expanded since their early development in the 19th century, many people find that giving attention to their psychological wellbeing is crucial to their spiritual development. Whilst some psychological schools are atheistic, many are deeply spiritual. In this respect, several of our biographers mention the influence of Carl Jung and the need for self-discovery.

'A phase of self-discovery and exploration was launched and enhanced by choosing to do some further study in the form of a Diploma in Pastoral Counselling and an MTh in Applied Theology. The former opened up life changing reflection on my own story, especially the effects of my mother dying when I was five years old.' SUE

Psychology has throughout much of its development focused on pathology; however, a relatively new branch, Positive Psychology, studies the conditions for human flourishing, positive traits, resilience, and optimal functioning. It aims to improve the quality of life. Insights from Positive Psychology are being integrated into Christian thinking, particularly its research into the power of gratitude, an attitude well-aligned with the teachings of Christianity and other religions.

Contemporary Spiritual Movements

The last few decades have seen an exponential growth in contemporary spirituality that goes beyond as well draws from religious traditions. Often, people who are exploring beyond the bounds of traditional Christianity find stimulation and nurture through these movements, and there is much cross-fertilisation between them. We will look at these in Part 4.

Chapter 4: Evolving Christianity – key features

In this chapter, we will examine many of the key features of an emerging and evolving Christianity, which some see as the development of an alternative orthodoxy.

Phyllis Tickle is known for her insistence that what she called 'the great emergence' is essentially a coming reformation to rival the significant changes in Christianity that occurred in the sixth, eleventh, and sixteenth centuries. *The Great* Emergence, and '*Emergence* Christianity' detail her sense that Christianity is on the verge of a transition to rival the Protestant Reformation of 500 years ago.[1]

It is suggested that a new or alternative orthodoxy is being born in Christianity today, spearheaded by writers and leaders such as Episcopalian priest, Cynthia Bourgeault, former monk, James Finley, and Fr Richard Rohr – names that featured in many of the biographies.

Those who embrace this shift see a return to the life and teachings of Jesus, believing that church and society have strayed from the meaning of the teachings and model provided in the life of Jesus as handed down to us. They postulate that it is not something new but a return to the essence of Christianity as taught by Jesus. According to James Finley, 'The Alternative Orthodoxy is the orthodoxy of the intimacy of love that breaks our heart open to see how unexplainably precious we are.'[2]

This alternative orthodoxy is characterised as evolutionary, inclusive, incarnational and heart-centred. A broad characterisation of the Alternative Orthodoxy can be viewed as a shift in focus from the doctrine of Atonement to at-one-ment. It contrasts from the prevailing view, which has been heard for many centuries, that atonement in terms of the sacrificial death of Jesus was to redeem those who believe in Him from the penalty of a hereafter in Hell. Instead, it sees the death of Jesus as changing our minds about God, to align with God, energised and motivated by the divine energy working within us, rather than by mind-driven ambitions or plans.

This is borne out by one of our biographers who found himself 'unable to believe in the Christian notion of redemption, 'which appeared to me to be about placating a vengeful god who demands the sacrificial death of the innocent man Jesus as the price of our salvation.' TIM

The new thinking in Christianity appeals to many Christians at the margins of the church, struggling within it or who have left, unable to find the life-giving essence of this original knowledge within it.

Some contemporary Christians are cautious about the term 'alternative orthodoxy,' because they associate the term orthodoxy with unhelpful dogma. Yet, whilst not espousing the term, many contemporary writers are expressing the values that can be found in it – inclusivity, the importance of humanity, care for the earth and each other, love as the fulfilment of the law, the importance of the heart.

1- New interpretations of the nature of Jesus of Nazareth

A number of biographers referred to their relationship to Jesus as having been, or remaining as, central to their faith. For some, this relationship had become less important and yet for others, new understandings of the nature and life of Jesus have deepened their relationship.

Jesus the Christ

In recent decades, there has arisen a re-examination and exploration of the life and teachings of Jesus. One area of re-evaluation relates to the way he is named, with some contemporary scholars suggesting that Jesus should more properly be referred to as Jesus the Christ rather than Jesus Christ. Christ is a designation rather than a name. There has been a teasing apart of the two names in wrestling with this idea. Jesus refers to the person who lived two thousand years ago, and the Christ refers to an energy of huge import and proportions, which Jesus was imbued with as in the following quote from Catholic priest and author Fr Richard Rohr: 'Jesus, by himself, does not have so many levels and seeming contradictions, and thus he is much easier to understand and to imitate than Christ. That is why Jesus is so necessary and important as a complement to Christ. He is like the grounding wire that holds this huge force field of Christ onto the earth, into concrete and personal experience, and into a consistent, moral worldview.'[3]

The Christ

Richard Rohr suggests that 'Christ, as such, is not precisely a religious principle, and certainly does not validate any organized or systematic religion. Christ is a life principle – the ubiquitous confluence of matter and spirit. Whenever we let such a wonderful recognition affect us, we have just met the Christ (and we don't need to call it Christ for it to be the true experience of Christ.).'[4] He postulates that we can connect with this same consciousness, 'this huge force field of Christ' through a process of letting go and embracing the universality of 'Christ Consciousness.'[5] In Rohr's thinking, and that of many contemporary Christian thinkers, The Christ or Christ-consciousness is not limited to being experienced only within Christianity.

In the New Testament letter to the Ephesians, a grand cosmic unification is alluded to, 'as a plan for the fullness of time, to unite all things in him (Christ), things in heaven and things on earth.'[6]

Many people today relate to concepts like Christ-consciousness, or experience the presence of Christ. However, this experience is not limited to people within the Church and is sometimes experienced by people of other faiths. For many now, it seems to relate more to a quality of being and/or a quality of relating positively and respectfully, which includes a sense of openness.

It is experienced as an inner energy or dynamism that shapes a person's actions in the world. Sometimes there is a sense of this being part of the world's evolutionary progress that is somehow aligning with this dynamic energy, which is part of the unfolding future of our world and cosmos, a sense of deep connection with all that is, the source of all being.

Others take heart and inspiration from the vision that all things will be reconciled and brought into harmony with one another in Christ, as expressed in some of the letters of the New Testament. Others see the early development of cosmopolitanism growing from Paul's writing and his insistence on there being neither Greek nor Jew nor slave nor free but all being one in Christ. This seemed to raise the status of the individual within the context of community in a society where people were often viewed as goods rather than as persons.

Referring Fr Richard Rohr again, 'The Christ Mystery is indeed "the way, the truth, and the life," but this is not about a religion or group one can join (which is how we have heard it), but rather a mystery of Incarnation that can be experienced by all, and in a million different ways.'[7]

The person, Jesus

The nature of Jesus has become a subject of new thinking and exploration. The debate about ascriptions such as Son of God and Son of Man continues. Questions about how much others can share in this nature abound. Here we will look at two prevalent contemporary understandings.

Wisdom Teacher

A wisdom teacher is someone who is able to lead people towards inner transformation and therefore new ways of living. Their teaching is embodied in how they themselves live. William Redfield suggests that 'Jesus was primarily known as a Wisdom teacher, being referred to as a 'moshelim,' which is a master of Wisdom. Jesus frequently taught in parables and Wisdom sayings called 'mashal.' Redfield points out that Jesus seemed to be 'the epitome of Wisdom, moving through life with a heart overflowing with compassion, generosity, and love.'[8]

Wisdom is characterised as embodied knowledge that links heart and mind. A wisdom teacher has the ability to let go of their individual conditioned thinking and be deeply attentive to what is arising in the moment. These abilities produce space where new insights can arise. Redfield points out that while some listeners were able to grasp the depth and breadth of the wisdom teaching of Jesus and his actions, many did not, and even the people, 'who did at times seem to get a grasp of the Wisdom he was conveying, were not always able to maintain it.'[9]

A wisdom teacher is one who can lead people to experience a transformation of their life, not just intellectual knowledge or belief. This is borne out in the very title of Cynthia Bourgeault's book, *The Wisdom Jesus*, with its strapline of *Transforming heart and mind*.

Political figure/social reformer who threatened social norms

Another widely read Christian thought-leader, Marcus Borg, has suggested that both the teaching and actions of Jesus reflect an 'alternative social vision.'

'Jesus was not talking about how to be good and how to behave within the framework of a domination system. He was a critic of the domination system itself.'[10]

This understanding of Jesus is reflected in many of the biographies. They show that one of the essential shifts is that of moving from a faith based on individual salvation and living largely within the confines of the institutional church, to a new understanding that embraces a vision for the whole of humanity and all life on planet earth. As Magda found: 'Collective salvation is redeeming the earth from the conditions that impoverish and prematurely kill millions of people, or deprive them of a life worth living, and the restoration of our beautiful planet have taken centre stage, and I feel most closely connected with the Source of all when working towards these ends.'

2- Non-duality, mysticism and the Unitive path

Here we will take a brief look at how the term 'non-duality' is increasingly used and how this relates to contemporary experiences beyond and within the Christian tradition.

'Non-duality (or non-dualism) is a way of living life, whereby, in each moment, you feel your interconnectedness with everyone and everything around you.'[11]

The term 'non-duality' was unfamiliar in the Christian tradition until quite recently when it entered through dialogue with other faiths. It is still relatively little-known, but it does link with the more traditional contemplative Christian path known to mystics. Non-duality is a term from Sanskrit that means 'not two.' In Eastern philosophy, it tends to relate to the experience of there being only one consciousness, with the emphasis placed on the sense of being an individual self, dissolved.

While non-duality is derived from the teachings of Advaita Vedanta, which is a Hindu spiritual path, it is also found within spiritual traditions around the world, including Western Christian and neo-Platonic traditions, as well as Buddhism.

Non-duality in Christianity

Whilst the term 'non-duality' is less frequently used within Christianity, in fact several of our biographers have been influenced by it. Non-duality in Christianity tends to have a different emphasis to that found in Indian philosophy: there is a greater focus on distinctiveness within the one consciousness as mentioned succinctly by Janet: 'I was being increasingly drawn to this more unitive consciousness (which some call non-dual spirituality), which embraces the paradox of being uniquely the person I am whilst simultaneously being one with all. I'm a drop in the ocean and the ocean is in the drop.'

Kate also mentions her experience of it: 'Perhaps one day I will wake up embedded in the consciousness of non-duality that I know to be there but keep slipping out of. Perhaps that is the end of the journey.'

Fr Bruno Barnhard alludes to a reason why the term is not well known to Christians: 'Unitive reality lives at the heart of the Western spiritual traditions, but it has rarely been expressed there with the directness and purity with which we find it in the Hindu and Buddhist literature.'[12]

In Christianity, non-duality tends to be expressed in terms of mysticism or the Unitive Path, and there are subtle differences in how it is experienced within the Christian tradition when compared with Eastern traditions, which espouse the experience of emptiness. A growing number of Christians who are exploring and embracing a nondual or mystical path are often, as we see in the biographies, stimulated by deep experiences of love and a sense of the Oneness of life.

Influential Christian mystic and teacher, Cynthia Bourgeault, describes 'Christian non-dual experience' in the following simple way: 'To perceive oneself as one with everything is to directly experience the flow of divine abundance that holds everything together.'[13]

She also argues that there are important nuances within a Christian understanding of non-duality: insights drawn from an incarnational viewpoint, that non-duality should not be seen as a retreat into a state of ecstasy but can lead to an understanding of 'not one, not two, but one and two.'[13]

Magda hints at this understanding in her biography: 'I believe that love requires a synthesis of the non-dualism of union with God and the dualism of relationship with and within The Divine.'

Fr Richard Rohr relates the unitive experience to the life of Jesus, equating it in part to the ability to see beyond the surface to the essence. He movingly describes the way in which Jesus saw people and situations through a unitive lens. 'He saw the Kingdom of Heaven even "in the midst" of the Pharisees; he saw the real woman behind the label of Samaritan; he saw the thief on the cross with him in paradise.'[14] (Richard Rohr, paradise.'[14] (Daily Meditations, 28th March 2015)

3- Spiritual Practices and the importance of the heart

Spiritual Practices:

Although there has been a decline in the west of organised institutionalised religion, an enormous increase in spiritual practices has accompanied it. Some of these are being adopted and even taught by people who have no belief in a Divine being. These practices create connection with nature, with others, with God or a higher power, and when people connect in this way, they tend to have a greater sense of wellbeing. In the last few decades, spiritual practices have been the subject of numerous scientific studies that have shown that when meditating, certain parts of the brain begin to become less active, which can lead to receptivity at a deeper level of consciousness. This can be experienced as transformative.

There has been a huge growth in a variety of practices including a revival of Pilgrimage and development of pilgrimage infrastructure such as the route to Compostela. Other growing practices include consciously connecting with and immersing oneself in nature, the practice of silence and stillness, including Centering Prayer and meditation, Lectio Divina (contemplative reading of scripture/sacred writings), and attending Choral Evensong, online or in person. Christians are increasingly adopting practices such Mindfulness, Yoga, Tai Chi and Qigong.

The Importance of the heart in Spiritual Life

Practices such as those mentioned above awaken our hearts, which can then deepen our sense of reality of the dimension of spirit.

'The spiritual journey, in Christianity as well as non-Christian forms, is about the hatching of the heart, the opening of the self to the reality of the Spirit. This opening begins the process by which the self at its deepest level is reoriented and transformed."[15] (Marcus Borg Legacy website.)

Ancient wisdom has long recognised that meaningful life is deeply connected with our hearts and emotions, where wisdom and courage are contained. In the past twenty or thirty years, research has shown that the heart is much more than a physical organ that sustains life by pumping blood around the body. The HeartMath Institute research suggests that the heart is a complex centre for processing information, which reacts to stimuli before the brain does. It communicates with the brain via the nervous and hormonal systems as well as by other means.[16] It has also been shown that the heart has a strong magnetic field that radiates out of the body and can influence people within its range. There are many different levels through which we can relate to or awaken our hearts and the gifts this has to offer.

It can enable us to adopt a multi-partial and nonviolent approach to conflict and suffering, not taking sides or being neutral but seeking to stand with all who are suffering, oppressed or facing injustice regardless of racial origins, religious beliefs, political ideology, or which side of a conflict they are engaged in.

There is a certain spaciousness and softening within the wisdom of the heart that enables a vision of and connection with the whole web of life and this connection allows us to act wisely. Working for the flourishing of all, with all its joy, obstacles and at times weariness, our heart energy is an important wellspring to sustain and nourish us. All these qualities relate to the awakening to Oneness and universality that many Christians are experiencing today. As we go into deeper levels of the heart, we connect more deeply with all that is.

Cynthia Bourgeault describes the heart as 'an organ of spiritual perception' and this also chimes with the research of the HeartMath Institute mentioned above. In an important book by Anne Hillman, there is further recognition of the power and intelligence of the Heart: 'The hope for any real change in our lives lies in the awakening of the human heart and mind. Such an awakening transforms the quality of all our relationships... we may come to embody a different kind of Love, one that has long been misunderstood. This kind of Love is not a feeling; it is a great power – an intelligence which has long been present inside us.'[17]

4- Creation spirituality and ecology

'Many people today are calling for modern religion, and specifically Christianity, to be re-imbedded in the cosmos, so that religion might become a real force in providing the ethical and spiritual energy for the critical task of reversing the degradation of the Earth.'[18] Vincent Rossi (Eastern Orthodox environmentalist and theologian, quoted in an article by Margaret Barker)

There is a growing urgency for all religions to come together to reverse the degradation of the earth. This urgency is reflected in Christianity in a renewed appreciation of the earth and a desire to protect and restore it.

Creation-centred spirituality, Green Spirit, and deep ecology movements are amongst those leading the way. They represent a shift from seeing the divine reflected in creation to seeing that the divine is immanent within each cell of nature and that we need to respect and uphold the sacredness of the environment without which we could not live. Many are re-embracing Mother Earth/Nature, often in the concept of Gaia, which sees the earth and its inhabitants as a living system deserving of our utmost respect. In creation spirituality, creation itself is embraced as sacred, a text revealing the Presence of God.

The indigenous traditions have long held this knowing. 'What man does to the earth he does to himself,' said Chief Seattle to the colonisers moving west across native lands. The understanding is causing people to grasp that deep ecology and contemporary Christianity need to walk hand in hand.

5- The Common Good - Social Justice

Fr Diarmuid O'Murchu, who kindly wrote the Foreword to this book, stresses that 'Christian discipleship today is evolving, beyond the admiration for, and worship of, a divine patriarchal hero, into a collaborative endeavour for empowering love and justice, fired by the radical vision of the New reign of God...'[19]

Integral to a more universal perspective is the widening of our circle of concern and compassion beyond our immediate family, friends and community. Many Christians find in the teachings and actions of Jesus the imperative of loving your neighbour as yourself. Now there is an increasing awakening to seeing his teachings as pointing in the direction of love for all people, and seeing the whole of humanity as our neighbours, to be treated with positive regard and compassion regardless of colour, class, creed, age, gender or sexual orientation. This is all very challenging – as G. K. Chesterton observed, the problem with Christianity is that it has been found difficult and not tried!

Many individuals and groups are now sensing a call from God to use their energies in working together for a world in which all people can flourish, to be at the service of humanity as a whole. The term 'Social Justice Christians' has arisen in recent decades. This awareness is felt most clearly in the growing numbers of people who are finding in Christ's teachings the call to become more fully human and deeply engaged with co-creating a new world. In the process, many of our old ways of doing things are being broken down or radically changed together with the institutions that embodied them.

Dr Martin Luther King, Baptist minister and US Civil rights leader, urged people to build a 'beloved community,' a community that works for the empowerment and upliftment of each member, beyond any single religious tradition or race.

'Dr King's Beloved Community is a global vision in which all people can share in the wealth of the earth. In the Beloved Community, poverty, hunger and homelessness will not be tolerated because international standards of human decency will not allow it. Racism and all forms of discrimination, bigotry and prejudice will be replaced by an all-inclusive spirit of sisterhood and brotherhood.'[20]

This impulse was echoed in Jill's biography: 'My inspiration are all those people who are doing Christ's work today, wherever they are found inside or outside churches – they are the ones who, by sacrificing themselves, will save the world.'

Together with many of the parables of Jesus, the Sermon on the Mount is a supreme scripture that espoused the common good. In Matthew chapter 25, the blessed are those who have fed the hungry, clothed the naked, visited those who are sick and those in prison.

Contemplative Social Action is an approach that can resource those who serve, as a buffer against burnout and it helps towards the personal transformation needed to become more a part of the solution than of the problem. Contemplative practices can nourish and sustain when the going gets tough, as it almost inevitably does, as we honestly face and engage more deeply and positively with the chaos and inequality in our world.

6- Theology and the Scriptures

Theological study is a vast discipline that has occupied the hearts and minds of scholars and believers for centuries. New scholarship and interpretations are constantly adding to our knowledge and are the subject of lengthy and often heated debates and weighty tomes. Here we can only briefly highlight a couple of aspects that are especially relevant to the themes in this book.

In terms of Scripture, an issue that has come more to the fore in recent decades relates to the canon and authority of Christian Scripture, sparked by the discovery of the Nag Hamadi Library and other texts that had remained hidden for centuries. The Nag Hamadi Library consists of fifty-two texts written in Coptic, discovered in a cave near the village of Nag Hamadi in 1945. Many of these texts had been unknown in modern times. These gospels are often referred to as Gnostic Gospels because they are deemed to be authored by Gnostic Christians in the early centuries after the time of Jesus, some possibly older than the gospels in The Bible. The term 'gnostic' refers to a certain kind of inner knowing based on personal or mystical experience, often induced through rituals, and is itself also the subject of much debate.

Some see the so-called Gnostic gospels as fraudulent and heretical, and others see them as casting new light on the teachings of Jesus and the early church. Of the gospels that were found, perhaps the most widely known is the Gospel of Thomas, and at least one of our biographers refers to being influenced by it. This gospel contains a series of teachings described as the hidden teachings of Jesus, perhaps those mentioned in the Biblical gospels as those Jesus taught to a few followers who could understand them. Many Christians do find helpful learning from this gospel and others that come under the term Gnostic. For more information, a good starting place would be *The Gnostic Gospels* by Elaine Pagels, an American historian of religion and Professor of Religion at Princeton University.[21]

In terms of theology, which is sometimes regarded with suspicion by believers who are not academically minded, it might be helpful to note that theological thinking is often prophetic, hatching new understandings before they become generally available and later adopted in the wider community. Often these ideas are initially surprising and cause consternation but, years later, they become accepted, and this is a significant part of the evolution of Christian belief and tradition.

7- New Christian Movements and sources of belonging

Before we dive into this section, it's important to remember that, as noted in the Introduction, many of the challenges and changes Christianity and particularly the institutional church is facing are not specific to the Church, or only to religious institutions, but are true for institutions in society in general. One such aspect is the erosion of a sense of community and belonging. This needs to be urgently addressed, as people become more and more individualised and society becomes more polarised.

So much of what held people together in the Western

world no is longer a part of our post-modern society. Many membership organisations are losing and finding difficulty in recruiting members. There is rising distrust in our institutions of government, economics, law and medicine. Together with growing distrust in our large corporations, and the rise of oligarchy and authoritarian leadership in many Western countries, people can often find themselves rudderless and not knowing which way to turn, how to find truth or tackle the urgency for sustainability and regeneration of all life.

The Church has traditionally brought people together in the community and for the Church to grow again and increase its relevance, part of the answer will lie in offering authentic communities and hospitality. There is a need to belong in local communities, and the challenge for the institutional Church is to meet this need, in a way that is hospitable, inspiring and empowering wherever people are in their journey of faith.

'The renewal of both the Church and Society will come through the re-emergence of forms of Christian community that are homes of generous hospitality, places of challenging reconciliation and centres of attentiveness to the living God.'[22] (Brother Samuel SSF, quoted in *A New Monastic Handbook: From Vision to Practice*, Ian Mobsby and Mark Berry)

Meeting together is an important part of most spiritual paths, whether by sharing in singing, chanting, study, in conviviality, or in relationships. For many people who have perhaps fled to the margins of Christianity, it has been problematic to find a group in their locality where they can feel at home, feel nurtured, inspired, and energised.

However, Kate points to a reason why the church continues to meet important needs in a comprehensive way, 'I continue to travel with Christianity because, despite all I have learnt from the East and from more esoteric ways of thought, it still provides me with the most comprehensive and inclusive philosophy that embraces light and dark, materiality and spirituality, joy and sorrow, and gives meaning through the transforming power of love to the anguish and the pain we see all around us'.

8- New Ways of Meeting Together and The Rise of Online/Internet Church

The Internet has become increasingly important, and peoples' connections are becoming global as well as local. Many people have become global figures by associating with networks that allow local groups to form so that people can find nourishment and kinship within a more local context as well as the inspiration of the well-known figurehead. It seems that this is one of the ways in which the alternative orthodoxy is taking route. For example, several of the biographers mentioned contemporary Christian teachers such as Richard Rohr, Cynthia Bourgeault and Matthew Fox, each of whom have websites and offer online events. Some even send out daily meditations.

Many Christians have been re-energised through meeting over the Internet with like-minded people around the globe. For example, Zoom allows conversation where a leader will speak or panel will discuss and then open the session to wider audience participation. A sense of solidarity and connection and hope develops through these. Meeting and hearing voices of other Christians around the globe who are thinking in similar ways and looking for the same kinds of changes is empowering, hopeful and energising.

Other sources of inspiration and help are the courses being run today, whether online or in person. Adult Christian learning is an important feature of what is emerging – the opportunity to learn in a more open-ended way allows one's experience to be tested against different wisdoms, whether ancient, contemporary and/, local or global. This often takes place through Retreat Houses, para-church networks, in forums or through online courses.

9- Ecumenism

Many people finding and even returning to Christian roots are at the same time investigating and exploring beyond their local church or traditional Christian belief, in the wider fields of interfaith, inter-spirituality, and ecumenism. They are finding that their journeys cannot be within one tradition, or are not held or met by it, but come alive at the confluence of several different places, groups, and traditions. They are also seeking inspiration and teachings that enable them to connect more deeply with the heart of the world rather than feeling confined to one group.

Partly because of the decline in church attendance, as well as a movement beyond previous boundaries and delineations of separate church traditions, a more ecumenical Christianity has developed relatively recently. An example of this is Churches Together in Britain and Ireland, which strives for churches to 'work more together, less apart.' Interestingly its London address is 'Interchurch House.'

10- Spiritual Accompaniment

There has been the growth in the practice of spiritual accompaniment, where individuals train to accompany others on their spiritual journey. This is not 'therapy' but does involve deep, non-judgemental listening on the part of the accompanier to help the other person to connect with their inner being and the 'still, small voice of Spirit in their lives.' Many retreat houses and dioceses offer this practice and, in the case of the latter, will offer both training to people who feel a calling to accompany others as well as help people to connect with an appropriate accompanier. This practice enables people to listen deeply to themselves, hear the Spirit within, explore beyond previous formulations and challenge their own assumptions. It is a supportive process that facilitates growth.

This is enormously helpful in a path of growth and transformation and can alleviate some of the loneliness experienced during times of transition and re-examination.

Magda wrote, 'There was isolation and loneliness as internally I felt more and more adrift from the beliefs and often the way of life of the groups I had felt so much a part of. The way sometimes seemed dark as a sense of unknowing enveloped me, yet even within the most difficult times something would 'crop-up' to guide me – a word that brought inklings of a new direction and fresh insights.'

So, in this chapter we have briefly examined several factors and changes that can be found in Western Christianity, which are leading to a more Universal understanding and expression of faith. Later we will make some recommendations for further exploration on these topics, which we have barely been able to skim the surface of here. Also, a list of new movements, websites and centres will be given at the end of the book.

PART FOUR

The Future Emerging

Chapter 1: Beyond Christianity – the Challenge and Opportunity of Contemporary Spiritual Movements

'...is there an inherent role for spirituality and religion from the innate reservoir of human wisdom that forms the underpinning of our species' millennial history – albeit obscured by a plethora of social and cultural factors?'[1] (Kurt Johnson and David Robert Ord)

This chapter is a brief introduction to the field of contemporary spiritual groups and movements, some of which are for people who are not finding their needs met in traditional churches. There is often an overlap between their aims, goals and practices with traditional faiths. However, there are also some sharp divergences such as being relatively free from dogma and having less emphasis on long-term or even lifetime commitments. At the end of this book, we will provide a resource list of some of these groups and movements for further exploration. It's a large field, which is difficult to adequately cover in a single chapter. We introduce them here as many of our biographers have been influenced by these movements, finding in them nurture and expansion of consciousness or belief that resonates with the processes and change occurring both in their lives and in the wider world.

As Janice says in her biography, 'I can no longer look backwards at an historical Christianity but feel called instead to listen to the summons of Christ – now – in present time. Instead of joining my local Church community I feel called to be part of the many communities and small groups that have started worldwide in the last few decades and are now linking up.'

Although church attendance and allegiance in most of the Western world has sharply declined, it does not signify a lack of hunger for what may be described as the depth of the spiritual dimensions of life. Many who can no longer feel nourished through traditional or perhaps institutional religion are seeking communion, community and sustenance elsewhere.

Some of this need is met by the growth in inter-spiritual and other spiritual movements, which assist people both in a quest for deeper meaning in life and engagement with the urgent and devastating problems posed by climate change, conflict, polarisation, and rising violence. Many of these movements are transnational, aided enormously by the rise of the internet in a similar way to that mentioned above in the section on emerging Christianity.

These movements, some of which initially focussed on individual wellbeing and spiritual development, increasingly have a focus on becoming co-creators of a just and sustainable world. They often have one charismatic leader at the helm, who supplements their own teaching and ideas with guest presenters aligned with their thinking. Although they are sometimes unable to offer in-person events, they do try to create a sense of global community by providing online forums.

An example of a contemporary spiritual thought-leader is Mirabai Starr, who identifies herself as inter-spiritual, but is also an acclaimed writer on Christian Mystics. It is not uncommon for such leaders to draw on the teachings of many traditional faiths as well as contemporary thought. As we accept the rich diversity of expressions of spirituality, we may find the love, the beauty, goodness, and truth at the heart of every path, and they will collectively be able to provide a secure 'rock' on which to build a shared future.

Often at the heart of these movements, there is an emphasis on spiritual or reflective practices, some of which can be found within traditional Christianity and other faiths, and some derived from Indigenous and Eastern traditions. As previously mentioned there has been a huge rise in meditation practices in traditional faiths, and these practices are central to contemporary, non-faith-based movements. In medical and business environments, meditation is used to gain clarity, for the alleviation of anxiety, and stress relief.

Ground-breaking and renowned scientist, Rupert Sheldrake, has authored two books on spiritual practices, *Science and Spiritual Practices* and *Ways to go Beyond and Why they Work*.[2] In both books, he explores and highlights the value of a wide variety of spiritual practices, both within traditional religious frameworks and beyond them. In the latter book he explores how to experience states of bliss, higher consciousness, love and compassion and the practices that can induce them. Whilst Rupert Sheldrake is a committed Anglican, both books make spiritual practices available to all, seeing them as part of our common human heritage.

Many groups seek to meet the hunger for meaning by nurturing a way of being in the world which connects to the depth dimensions of life, beyond traditional beliefs and dogmas, fostering a sense of Oneness, a sense that we are all in this together with the will to work to contribute to a world which works for all.

Challenges facing contemporary spiritual movements

For the new spiritual movements outside of formal religions, there is an enormous challenge in being able to meet the need for local, face-to-face community. Few of them are able to offer a living, local community which can nurture all ages as does the institutional church, or longstanding groups such as the Quakers or the various Universalist Churches. Meeting online, whilst providing nourishing global connections, does not meet the heartfelt desire for sustaining, local, face-to face relationships with likeminded people. There needs to be the possibility of communities coming together to co-create spiritual centres focussing on renewal and restoration and offer space that welcomes all people to be quiet, to converse and to worship the

Supreme Source and Sustainer of all life, however they may deem this to be.

A further challenge for new movements is that they can appear elitist because of their need to offer their teaching and services for people who are sufficiently well-off to pay the fees and are time-rich enough to take part in their programmes. The possibility of hybrid, part online, part in person, events help to meet this challenge. Some groups hire church buildings and other venues, unable to have their own, as finances are limited. For some this is a specific choice to avoid becoming institutionalised whilst exploring new ways of organising themselves.

Many of the contemporary spiritual movements understand that we are living through a state of flux and are 'going with the flow', seeing the ever-changing landscape of spirituality not just as a challenge but as an invitation to evolve in more expansive ways. This could involve collaborating with others, deeply listening to our culture, and acting in alignment with the Spirit in all things. 'The wind blows where it wishes, and you hear the sound of it, but you cannot tell where it comes from or where it goes. So is with everyone who is born of the Spirit.'[3]

Trends in contemporary spiritual movements

In summary, the current trends in contemporary spirituality seem to be moving in several directions:

The first is an expansion of a worldview from one of separation to one that embraces the growing unity consciousness.

Many people are more deeply embracing expanded perspectives as well as the reality of other dimensions of being such as the angelic realms.

The second is the realisation that each of us has an inner life awaiting our discovery and nurture. This trend towards connection with the 'God within' is fundamental at the Findhorn Foundation that was cited by several of the biographers. This is perhaps being indicated by the increasing popularity of mindfulness and meditation practices.

Third, there need to be movements that can speak to younger people, meeting their concerns and speaking in a language that communicates to their hearts. Many youngsters resort to the myriad of distractions modern technology provides to shield them from a fear of a future which they apprehend as, in many ways, doomed. They tend to be put off by communities which are in effect closed systems, with rigid beliefs that do not allow for the emergence of new ideas.

A fourth trend is that of a growing hunger to discover the deeper meaning of life and search for sustenance that the mainstream press mostly ignores. This has led to the growth of spiritually minded magazines such as *Resurgence and Ecologist*, which is over forty years old (4), '*Positive* News,'(5) which provides articles on the positive initiatives around the world (and *Caduceus*, which brings us up to date with spirituality and healing.[4]

Charity-supported Centres for Adult Education offer workshop programmes, lectures, conferences and opportunities

□

for dialogue, particularly for young people who are needing an approach and language that speaks to the present time and to their souls.

Chapter 2: A Relevant Spirituality

'A post-secular society is marked by recognition that religion is once again important.'[1]

Traditional religions, including Christianity and the new spiritual movements, are being challenged in these times to develop a spirituality and framework relevant to current developments in human learning and the world situation. Perhaps it has never been more so than now, with the expansion of knowledge and rate of change have been as rapid as they are now. An authentic spirituality needs to speak to people's inmost needs as well as the crises and concerns of the age. Drawing on the biographies, and the exploration in this book, here is a summary of some factors that faith and spirituality need to recognise if they are to be relevant in contemporary times.

The need for deeper connection

There emerged for many a growing understanding, now evidenced by leading-edge science, that all life is deeply interconnected so that all religions could be seen as parts of the same whole.

The mystics of ancient India also saw this and proclaimed the concept of Indra's net, which, like a subtle matrix, held all the interconnections of the web of life with nodal points shining like jewels, each reflecting the whole. Jesus described it in a different way, praying 'that they all may be one, as You, Father, are in Me, and I in You; that they also may be one in Us.'[2] Many people have felt isolated, at least for a period, as their beliefs transformed and this led to a yearning to connect with kindred spirits.

A need for silence and receptivity

For those living in cities with a constant buzz of noise and activity, external silence can be much harder to find than for those living in rural areas. Some may seek a quiet space inside a church, although many churches today are locked when there is no service underway, or no one is available to be present, partly due to incidents of theft or vandalism.

To address the need for contemplation and silence, many churches offer smaller services outside the main busier and louder gathering. Cathedrals often offer quiet space in a side chapel, but there is rarely scope for this in smaller churches. Some are setting aside times for prayer and contemplation, and one Anglican priest established a network of open quiet gardens for this purpose.[3] As highlighted earlier, there is huge growth in Christian networks fostering contemplative approaches.

Beyond church and cathedral, several of the biographers spoke of how they were drawn to spend time at the Findhorn

Foundation, where regular times of meditation and silent group attunements are held before any activity. It was being in the silence that helped them to live more fully in the present moment either with their own reflections or those received by Eileen Caddy, one of the three co-founders of Findhorn. These inspirations are published in a small book called *Opening Doors Within*.[4]

A need to restore a balance between
the feminine and the masculine

Because many of the world's religions developed in times when patriarchy dominated the social order, most of the creeds, liturgies and traditions were established from a masculine perspective, which often focussed more on the rational, cognitive and forceful ways of thinking than the creative, imaginative and more receptive ways of the feminine spirit. This has led to God being 'He' and the voice of women generally being scripted out. Mary, the mother of Jesu,s was raised to a status above the ordinary human, but Mary Magdalene was, for many centuries, written off as a prostitute. Present research is correcting this practice and a recent publication based on scholarly research shows a very different role that Mary Magdalene played, as the companion of Jesus who understood his deeper teaching and became a teacher in her own right. She is now often referred to as an Apostle to the Apostles. Additionally, a book by the Episcopalian priest Cynthia Bourgeault, *The Meaning of Mary Magdalene*, gives us a deeper understanding of her contribution to the life and work of Jesus and her crucial role in the shifts now happening in Christian understanding.[5]

A need to move beyond an over-emphasis on belief

Jill mentions Gretta Vosper, who has spoken at meetings of the Progressive Christianity Network. Vosper's work 'bridges progressive Christianity and atheism, exploring beyond the boundaries of Christian thought. Her seminal book, *With or Without God,* argues for a post-Christian church where the way we live is more important than what we believe.'

There is arising a greater emphasis on orthopraxis, rather than belief, the need to be actively involved in care for all life on planet earth, with the way faith shapes our doing being of supreme importance.

The need to develop a deeper connection
with nature

In 2021, the global convergence on Glasgow for COP 26 highlighted for many the critical need to restore a relationship with the natural world, to move beyond seeing nature as a resource to be exploited for gain and profit and instead to conserve, sustain and revere all natural life. Early translations of the statement in the Book of Genesis, 'And God said, Let us make man in our image, after our likeness: and let them have dominion over the fish of the sea, and over the fowl of the air, and over the cattle, and over all the earth, and over every creeping thing that creepeth upon the earth'[6] has at times been interpreted in grossly misleading ways. Instead, there is now a growing understanding that what we need is a deep and loving connection. Mother Earth needs our stewardship and active regeneration. As previously mentioned, Pope Francis took the lead on this with the publication of his encyclical *Laudate Si* in 2015.[7]

The need for using appropriate language

We are certainly living through a time of transition where the language used could be adapted to better suit people of different backgrounds. A recent private survey of forty young people 18-30 years old from different countries meeting under the auspices of Wyse International, which runs programmes for potential young leaders, strongly indicated their preference that the word Spirit was fine, but spirituality was not because it sounded a bit religious; connection to Source was fine, God was not, because this word carried too much baggage.[8] Yet other young people are turning to more traditional and ancient expressions of faith such as that found in the Eastern Orthodox Church and some branches of Catholicism, **and conversions to Islam are booming.**

Language can easily divide those whose spirituality is strongly linked to religion and those who find and express it in more secular ways. There is a need to find common ground, tolerance and understanding that not all language will appeal to everyone. This requires openness and a willingness to engage with others who express themselves in terms that do not immediately resonate with us.

The need for a greater sense of heart and soul

A growing number of people are beginning to realise that science and technology do not have all the answers we desperately need. Crucial to developing a deeper sense of soul is the work of the heart, but there are good signs that a return to heart-centeredness is indeed occurring: 'Spiritual emphasis on the experience of "the heart" and states of unitive higher consciousness appear to nurture universally profound life-altering experiences of interconnectedness, mutuality and "Oneness".' These experiences are reflected in an increasingly expanding worldwide popular literature and media regarding the experience of a global collective or gestalt of 'We.'[9]

The depth of the soul or heart require time and a degree of quiet to fully emerge, and from this the wisdom so much needed now. However, there are good signs that numerous networks appreciate the path towards a deeper hearted response to life. One of these is The Scientific and Medical Network, who have for forty years explored the evolving edges of scientific understanding and have recently changed their strap line to 'Where evidence-based reasoning meets deep inner wisdom.'[10]

Linking the wisdom accessed when the heart and brain are in harness together with scientific discovery is a big step forward. It is propelling us towards more heart-centred living, increasing compassion towards others, and discovering love as the glue that binds all together, helping us to understand what Albert

Schweitzer first saw as the need to have 'reverence for all life.'[11]

Rediscovering the teachings of Jesus

Some of the biographers have shown how they now see traditional teachings in a way new for them, and this understanding has led to a more universal perspective. Take for instance the phrase that 'all of you are children of the Most High.'[12] If God is all love, all light, and all knowing, then in a lesser way we too must inherit these attributes or at least have within us the potential to develop them. The visionary Sir George Trevelyan, teaching from the early 1960s till his death in 1996, used to say, 'we are all droplets of divinity.'[13] This is a profound thought and akin to a teaching long held within the Eastern Orthodox tradition of theosis. Simply put, it is a process by which a person becomes increasingly one with God, which is the goal of the Christian life.

Perhaps many are beginning to glimpse the truth of the statement of Jesus, 'he who believes in Me, the works that I do he will do also; and greater works than these he will do.'[14]

Another aspect of rediscovery of the teachings of Jesus is the recent commitment to Christianity by several notable public figures such as Paul Kingsnorth, ecologist and writer, and Martin Shaw, mythologist and writer. It is too early yet to say whether this is the start of a new trend, but their voices are certainly influencing people through popular podcasts.

Collective and Global Needs

The need for a greater convergence between spirituality and science

There is a popular saying that 'those who understand quantum physics don't fully understand it,' which is some comfort for those of us faced with the new physics, epigenetics, consciousness research, evolutionary system design, cosmology, etc. we have never studied. Each frontier is now expanding rapidly. Nevertheless, we can be open to the new evidence of the scientific side of life as it moves forward, and trust that today's open-minded scientists do not meet the fate that earlier scientists such as Galileo and Copernicus endured in their day when their insights did not gain approval of the appointed ecclesiastical authorities.

The need for collective action

The present times seem to be calling for a more connected collective response to the current planetary polycrisis, where the crises in different systems are interrelating and impacting one another. Climate change, biodiversity loss, increasing financial global instability, growing polarisation, wars and mass migration of populations are bringing us to the brink of disaster.

We seek to move beyond our divisions and work together for much needed restoration and regeneration of all that is good and beautiful and true, and so bring about the fulfilment of the *Dream of the Cosmos* as outlined by Dr Anne Baring in her highly regarded book of this name, in which she describes, 'The dream of an enlightened humanity engaging in a new role on this planet: a role that is in harmony with the evolutionary intention of the Cosmos and is no longer driven by the quest for power, conquest and control and the appropriation of the Earth's resources for the benefit of the few. As we begin consciously to align ourselves with this luminous ground of reality, our minds will serve the deepest longing of our heart, the deepest wisdom of our soul. We will know who we are and why we are here.'[15]

Many of the biographers express the desire to work for the common good, to live out and embody the consciousness so many now experience of the Oneness underpinning all reality. People, whether within Christianity or beyond, are seeking an empowering vision, and a spirituality which is authentic, embraces the whole of life and can lead to transformation of self, community and planet. In short, a participative spirituality is needed that embraces people, planet and even the entire Cosmos with love.

How can the more universal understanding be embodied and expressed in our lives to address the grave issues humanity is facing? For each of us the 'how to' will be different, so in the final short chapter we present a meditation on a poem that can help us to reflect on our own spirituality and role in addressing the urgent issues we are facing at this critical time.

Chapter 3: Embodying a Loving Universal Perspective – A reflection

The teachings and life of Jesus demonstrate a universality and integral wholeness of love. In contemporary times, this begins to reveal itself to us in a new way so that our loving concern encompasses a greater whole than once it did. The Franciscan Sister, Ilia Delio, founded and steers the Center for Christogenesis in the USA and online, and draws on the work of the mystic priest, Pierre Teilhard de Chardin. The Center is a leading light in the search for a new holistic synergy of science. At the core of its work is the premise that love is the fundamental force in the universe affecting not just humans but the whole cosmic order. It was Teilhard de Chardin who famously wrote, 'Someday, after mastering the winds, the waves, the tides and gravity, we shall harness for God the energies of love, and then, for a second time in the history of the world, man will have discovered fire.'[1] As we begin to discover this fire, we find a creative new vision for our world and the part that each of us is being invited to play.

And so, as we come to the end of this book, we finish with a reflection on a poem by Janice Dolley, which explores the theme of being a bridge builder into the new and living with a more universal and loving awareness – not just awareness of mind but of heart, embracing the whole of life with love. Each stanza will be followed by relevant reflections. At the end of the chapter, the whole poem will appear. Then you may like to read it slowly and meditatively, allowing the words to take root while being open to new insights.

What is it to be a Bridge-Builder to the New?

It is to live in the full awareness of every moment
As a divine droplet of potentiality
In the ocean of eternity

This stanza speaks of an awareness of time rooted in the present moment but which also connects with eternity. Additionally, it recognises our inner divinity as part of the Incarnation (see *New Incarnation and Awareness of Deep Time*).

Suggested practice: Connecting with the Present Moment.

Take some minutes to still your mind through prayer, meditation, or even listening to peaceful music. Then begin to focus on the sounds around you, listen but do not become involved in thoughts about them. Next, become aware of the sense of touch, the seat you are sitting on, the touch of your clothes. Now become aware of the sense of smell, again opening your senses without judgement.

Rest in a sense of open awareness this practice may have brought to you.

It is to see every person as carrying
the Christ Light within them
And every situation as an opportunity for releasing
A little more of the shadows that keep
that Light from shining

It can be an enormous challenge when faced with cruelty or unacceptable demands, rejection and the like to see the Christ light. However, to live without judgement and to connect with the Source of all love (Universal Spirit/Christ) is what enables this to become a reality.

Suggested practice: Contemplating right relationship.

You may like to take some time to reflect on these words from Rumi and how they may apply in any difficult relationship or situations you may be facing:

'Out beyond ideas of wrongdoing and right doing,

there is a field. I'll meet you there.

When the soul lies down in that grass,

the world is too full to talk about.

Ideas, language, even the phrase "each other"

doesn't make any sense.'[2]

It is to listen innerly at all times and all places
to the next step ahead
It is trusting each step to reveal itself to us
Knowing that every need will be perfectly met

Trust is paramount and efficient though not always easy! It is helped along by a process of inner listening, through which we can align ourselves with Spirit, with our deepest hearts, and receive an inner knowing not based on mental strategising of what our next steps need to be. This inner knowing is characterised by a quiet sense of peace and rightness, and an embodied, felt sense of what is needed at any given moment with a gentle sense of stability.

Suggested practice: Discerning the next best step.

Spend some time thinking of a question or practical situation you might be grappling with.

Then take some time to still yourself, slightly slowing your breathing. After a minute begin to visualise your breath flowing in and out through your heart centre in the middle of your chest. Once you have established this, begin to drop the question or situation into your awareness. Ask yourself, 'What is my deeper knowing about this?' Something might not emerge immediately, but be open to a new awareness, knowing or answer arising later.

It is embracing with loving arms
Those that appear to stand in the way of our purpose
As well as those who do not seem to understand
It is knowing that where two or three are gathered
The 'I am' presence is there in the midst

Those loving arms may be metaphorical or physical. Doing this requires us to remove the barriers to love in our own hearts. It also requires discernment. 'Embracing with loving arms' may mean different things at different times. There may be times when the best thing is to hold a person or situation in an energy of loving awareness while waiting to take action at that point.

The 'I am' presence refers to our alignment to the loving heart of all, the loving source of all being. We can enter this presence when we enter consciously into a loving field of energy.

Suggested practice: Loving-kindness meditation.

Take time to still yourself by whatever method works best for you. Then focus yourself as though breathing in and out through your heart. After a few minutes, focus on anything that gives you a feeling of being loved, and breathe with that sense. When you feel ready, extend that sense of love outwards to family, friends, and the whole world. Finish by returning to breathing with a sense of self-compassion and love, so that you can return to live rejuvenated and nourished by your practice.

It is embracing within our being the whole universe
Knowing that at one and the same time
Each of us is nothing and each of us is everything.

Humility is needed to realise our smallness in the order of things. Yet, we can also have confidence that comes from understanding that we embody everything because we are part of the Whole.

'Oneness' of course implies that we are all part of one body. Our connection to others is therefore important, and our relationship with all those we meet will define the way we are ourselves shaped.'[3] (Rev Daniel Costley)

Suggested practice: Meditation on our place in the whole.

Take some time to reflect on your place within, and your connection to, the great web of life. You may find the following words from Rev Daniel Costley helpful:

'And if we take God to be everything – something so vast and all containing that we are all a part of it, yet all such a tiny proportion, then the sense of Oneness with all creation becomes more real. It is only as a single world that we could possibly begin to understand the enormity of our collective possibility. Some might call that possibility God, others will not. But that intangible enormity that is life includes each and every one of us. And our neighbours. And our neighbour's neighbours. And on it goes."[4]

And here, for your enjoyment and contemplation, is the whole poem:

What is it to be a Bridge-Builder to the New?
It is to live in the full awareness of every moment
As a divine droplet of potentiality
In the ocean of eternity

It is to see every person as carrying
the Christ Light within them
And every situation as an opportunity for releasing
A little more of the shadows that keep
that Light from shining

It is to listen innerly, at all times, and all places
to the next step ahead
It is trusting each step to reveal itself to us
Knowing that every need will be perfectly met

It is embracing with loving arms
Those that appear to stand in the way of our purpose
As well as those who do not seem to understand

It is knowing that where two or three are gathered
The 'I am' presence is there in the midst

It is embracing within our being the whole universe
Knowing that at one and the same time
Each of us is nothing and each of us is everything.

POSTSCRIPT

As we come to the end of this book, we hope that you will find reflected in its pages, and especially the biographies, an all-embracing reach towards faith and spirituality. This is evident in the expressed desire for a more universal and evolutionary spirituality that can take into account past, present and future, one which is broad in its scope to encompass the whole cosmos and its story, as new discoveries reveal more of its dimensions and energy. In the words of two luminaries:

Thomas Berry in *Contemporary Spirituality*: 'There is no way of guiding the course of human affairs through the perilous course of the future except by discovering our role in this larger evolutionary process.'[1]

Sr Ilia Delio in *Contemporary Christianity*: 'As evolution continues and technology advances humankind, religions have to create new meaning together in the creation of a new global society of world citizens.'[2]

Resources

Exploring Christians moving towards Universal spirituality

Books:

Borg, Rev Marcus, The Heart of Christianity. New York (HarperCollins, 2003)

Bourgeault, Rev Cynthia, The Wisdom Jesus: Transforming Heart and Mind – a New Perspective on Christ and His Message (Shambhala Publications Inc., 2008)

Laird, Martin, Into the Silent Land – A Guide to the Christian Practice of Meditation. (Oxford University Press, 2006).

MacGregor, Don, Christianity Expanding: Into Universal Spirituality. (Christian Alternative Books, 2020)

O'Murchu, Diarmuid, Incarnation: A New Evolutionary Threshold (Orbis Books, 2017)

Rohr, Richard, The Universal Christ: How a forgotten reality can change everything we see, hope for and believe. (SPCK, 2019)

Smith, Adrian B., Tomorrow's Christian: A New Framework for Christian Living. (O Books, 2005)

Web resources and Organisations

The World Community for Christian Meditation
https://wccm.org/
'The WCCM is a global spiritual community united in the practice of meditation in the Christian tradition. It shares the fruits of this practice widely and inclusively, serving the unity of all and building understanding between faiths and cultures.'

Progressive Christianity Network
https://www.pcnbritain.org.uk/
A network with local groups, offering an invitation, not a set of answers, seeking a credible and inclusive way to follow Jesus, unafraid to question traditional church teaching and valuing contemporary thought and recent biblical understanding.

School for Christian Mysticism
http://www.schoolofchristianmysticism.co.uk/
A small but active online organisation meeting weekly to explore different ways of being Christian. Recent studies on The gospels of Thomas, Philip and The Beloved Companion have all bcome available as videos on their website.

The Unitarians https://www.unitarian.org.uk/
'We hold there are as many paths through life as there are people – and we help each other find our way. Together, we learn from

ancient wisdom, philosophy, science, art and poetry. We pray, meditate, find stillness in nature. We work on a common cause. We pay attention to our inner life; to what we see as sacred, holy'. They aim 'to promote a free and inquiring religion through the worship of God and the celebration of life; the service of humanity and respect for all creation; and the upholding of the liberal Christian tradition.'

The Contemplative Society https://www.contemplative.org/
'We are an inclusive non-profit society that encourages a deepening of contemplative practice based in the Christian Wisdom lineage, while also welcoming and being supportive of other spiritual traditions... We offer resources, recordings, and events led by our founding teacher Rev. Dr. Cynthia Bourgeault and other distinguished Wisdom teachers and leaders. We operate as part of a global Wisdom-focused network with a world-wide membership and following.'

Center for Contemplation and Action https://cac.org/
Based on the work of Fr Richard Rohr the Center for Action and Contemplation's programs and resources are designed to help deepen prayer practice and strengthen compassionate engagement in the world.

Living Spirituality Connections; Resources for Deeper Living
https://livingspirit.org.uk/

The purpose of Living Spirituality Connections is to encourage the mutual support of people exploring their own spiritual journeying amid new forms of spirituality. LSC will act as a resource for people to find material, groups and people to help deepen and anchor their spiritual explorations.

Center for Christogenesis https://christogenesis.org/
'seeks to deepen Pierre Teilhard de Chardin's integration of science and spirituality by providing insights and practices to enkindle awareness of love at the heart of reality'.

Creation Spirituality: Reawakening Mysticism. Protecting Mother Earth https://www.matthewfox.org/
Focuses on creation-centred spirituality and cognisant of the Sacred Feminine. 'Rooted in ancient Judeo-Christian tradition, supported by leading-edge science, bearing witness for social, environmental, and gender justice.'

CANA Christians Awakening to New Awareness https://www.cana.org
'Our hope is to rediscover and re-imagine a path leading towards a more universal spirituality that can operate with respect for all living creatures, a path of love and service for the betterment of all'

CANA videos https://www.cana.org.uk/videos/
A range of videos of their events for those exploring alternative

ways of looking at Christianity and expanding into universal spirituality.

More Christ YouTube Channel by Marcas Ó Conghaile Muirthemne
'...seeking to discern and share the beautiful, the good, and the true wherever I find it"it' and featuring highly acclaimed discussions with notable, well-known recent converts to Christianity.

Interfaith

Books:

Teasdale, Br. Wayne, *Discovering a Universal Spirituality in the World's Religions* (New World Library; New Edition 2001)

Starr, Mirabai, *God of Love: A Guide to the Heart of Judaism, Christianity and Islam* (Monkfish Book Publishing, 2019)

Web Resources and Organisations:

Parliament of the World's Religions
https://www.parliamentofreligions.org
'The Parliament of the World's Religions cultivates harmony among the world's spiritual traditions and fosters their engagement with guiding institutions in order to achieve a more *peaceful*, *just*, and *sustainable* world.'

□

World Congress of Faiths https://www.worldfaiths.org
'The World Congress of Faiths is open to all who share its aims and interests regardless of their faith. Our aim is to promote and share the personal values and public value of spiritual life.'

United Religions Initiative https://www.uri.org
'The purpose of the United Religions Initiative is to promote enduring, daily interfaith cooperation, to end religiously motivated violence, and to create cultures of peace, justice, and healing for the Earth and all living beings.'

Contemporary spirituality-beyond Christianity

Books:

Baring, Anne, *The Dream of the Cosmos: The search for the soul.* (Archive Publishing, 2013)

Kovacs, Betty, *Merchants of Light: The consciousness that is changing the world.* (The Kamlak Center, 2019)

Shapiro, Rami, *Perennial Wisdom for the Spiritually Independent: Sacred teachings annotated and explained.* (Skylight Paths Publishing, 2013)

Walsh, Roger, *Essential Spirituality: The 7 central practices to awaken heart and mind.* (John Wiley & Sons, 1999)

Web resources and organisations:

Scientific and Medical Network

https://scientificandmedical.net/

SMN is a creative international forum for lifelong transformative learning. It is part of a worldwide contemporary movement for assimilating spiritual understanding. They bring together scientists, doctors, psychologists, engineers, philosophers, complementary practitioners and other professionals in a spirit of open and critical enquiry, to explore frontier issues at the interfaces between science, consciousness, wellbeing and spirituality.

The Shift Network https://theshiftnetwork.com/

Their vision is to empower a global network of evolutionary change agents through media, education, and resources featuring leading wisdom keepers and visionaries. They empower people on a journey of personal growth over time, and provide a platform for an emerging culture to connect, collaborate, and co-create.

GreenSpirit https://www.greenspirit.org.uk/

Green Spirit is a network of people who celebrate the human spirit in the context of our place in the natural world and Earth's own evolutionary journey. Their radical vision brings together the rigour of science, the creativity of artistic expression, the passion of social action and the wisdom of spiritual traditions of all ages.

Attracting those of many faith traditions, they are a body of people who believe that human life has both an ecological and a spiritual dimension.

HeartMath Institute https://www.heartmath.org/
They hold the vision of 'A kinder, heart-centered world where we care for one another and live harmoniously in peace.'
'HeartMath's research, training and technologies are aimed at guiding all of humanity toward realization of its full potential and to rely on the qualities of the heart in its role as caretaker of future generations and our planet.'

Rupert Sheldrake https://www.sheldrake.org/audios/navigating-consciousness-podcast/
A wide-ranging discussion of consciousness at the intersection of science and spirituality with renowned Anglican scientist Rupert Sheldrake.

Buddha at the Gas Pump https://batgap.com/
Over 600 in-depth interviews with 'spiritually awakening people' from many different traditions.

Spirituality and Practice: Resources for Spiritual Journeys https://www.spiritualityandpractice.com/
The site's name reflects a basic understanding:
'*Spirituality* and *practice* are the two places where all the world's

religions and spiritual paths come together. While respecting the differences among traditions, we celebrate what they share in common.'

They offer online courses and other resources.

Ubiquity University https://www.ubiquityuniversity.org/

It is 'A Global University for Inner and Outer Regeneration.'

'Our integrated philosophy is a blend of learning experiences that range from the mystical to the practical. We keep one lens on the ancient past and the other on the coming future. You will find our approach as varied and unique as you are. We want to work with you to activate every intelligence in a holistic way so you are empowered to live your life with deeper understanding and purpose.'

Gangaji https://gangaji.org/

An invitation to shift your allegiance from the activities of your mind to the eternal presence of your being. Podcasts, videos, blogs with Gangaji.

100 Best Spiritual Blogs and Websites

https://blog.feedspot.com/spiritual_blogs/

Lots to explore here!

Bibliography

Part one

Introduction: The Landscape of Change

1: Dylan, B. (1964). The Times They Are A-Changin'. On The Times They Are A-Changin'. [Album]. Columbia Records.

2: Kaplan, G. S. (2020). Defining a New Leadership Model to Stay Relevant in Healthcare. *PubMed*. Retrieved from https://pubmed.ncbi.nlm.nih.gov/32079900/.

3: Berry, T. (1988). *The Dream of The Earth*. San Francisco: Sierra Club Books. (Reprint: Berkeley: Counterpoint, 2015)

Part two – Biographies

Chapter 1: The Importance of Personal Stories

Voices of Change:

1: Newman, J. H. (1845). *An Essay on the Development of Christian Doctrine*. Chapter 1, Section 1, Part 7.

Voices of Acceptance:

1: Rohr, R. (2016). *A Spring Within Us: A Book of Daily Meditations*. Albuquerque, NM: CAC Publishing.

2: Sofroniĭ, Archimandrite. (1958). *The Undistorted Image: Staretz Silouan, 1866-1938*. London: Faith Press.

3: Julian of Norwich. (1670). *Revelations of Divine Love* (S. de Cressy, Trans.).

4: Sereny, G. (1974). *Into That Darkness*. London: Andre

□

Deutsch Ltd.

5: Lawrence, D.H. (1977). *The Complete Poems of D. H. Lawrence*. New York: Penguin Books.

6: Lao Tzu. (n.d.). *Tao Te Ching*. Retrieved from Gutenberg.org.

7: Bourgeault, C. (2008). *The Wisdom Jesus: Transforming Heart and Mind – A New Perspective on Christ and His Message*. Publisher Location: Shambhala Publications.

8: Fox, M. (1994). *The Reinvention of Work: A New Vision of Livelihood for Our Time*. Publisher Location: Harper Press.

Voices of Discovery

1: Hopkins, G. M. (1954). *Poems and Prose*. Baltimore, Md: Penguin Books.

2: Jung, C. G. (1959). Face to Face [Television interview]. Interviewed by John Freeman. BBC.

3: Cummings, E. E. (1950). i thank You God for most this amazing day. *In Xaipe 1*. New York: Oxford University Press.

4: Rohr, R. *Definition of a Mystic*. Center for Action and Contemplation. Available at: https://cac.org/daily-meditations/incarnational-mysticism-2019-07-14/

5: Teilhard de Chardin, P. (n.d.). Pensees. *In Religion Online*. Retrieved from https://www.religion-online.org/book-chapter/chapter-4-pensees/.

6: Irenaeus. (c. 185 AD). *Against Heresies* (Lib. 4, 20, 5-7). In Crossroads Initiative. Retrieved from https://www.crossroadsinitiative.com/media/articles/man-fully-

□

alive-is-the-glory-of-god-st-irenaeus/.

7: Compston, K. (1990). *From Bread of Tomorrow: Prayers for the Church Year*. England.

8: Rohr, R. (2021, June 1). An Evolving Faith. In *Four Shapes of Transformation*. Center for Action and Contemplation. Retrieved from https://cac.org/daily-meditations/four-shapes-of-transformation-2021-06-01/.

Voices of Inspiration

1: Smith, A.B. (2004). *The God Shift: Our Changing Perception of the Ultimate Mystery*. Liffey Press.

Voices of Unity

1: Living Spirituality Connections. (n.d.). *Towards Human and Earth Flourishing*. Retrieved from https://livingspirit.org.uk/.

2: Rilke, R.M. (1929). *Letters to a Young Poet*. Insel Verlag.

3: Griffiths, B. (1976). *Return to the Centre*. Collins.

4: Halevy, Y. K. (2002). *At the Entrance to the Garden of Eden: A Jew's Search for God with Christians and Muslims in The Holy Land*. Perennial.

5: McFague, S. (1993). *The Body of God: An Ecological Theology*. Fortress Press.

6: O'Murchu, D. (2017). *Incarnation: A new Evolutionary Threshold*. Orbis Books.

Voices of Awakening:

1: Marx Hubbard, B. (2005). *Emergence: The Shift from Ego to Essence*. Walsch Books.

2: Blake, W. (1975). Auguries of Innocence. In Geoffrey Keynes (Comment.), John Sampson (Rearr.), *Auguries of Innocence*. The Cygnet Press, Burford, Oxfordshire.

3: PWheeler, E. (1883). *Poems of Passion*. Belford, Clarke & Co, Chicago.

4: Shakespeare, W. (2003). Hamlet. In Barbara A. Mowat & Paul Werstine (Eds.), *Hamlet* (Folger Shakespeare Library Series). Simon & Schuster.

5: Lorimer, D. (2003). *Radical Prince: The Practical Vision of the Prince of Wales*. Floris Books, Edinburgh.

6: Clarke, L. (2004). *Imagining Otherwise*. GreenSpirit Pamphlet No. 6.

7: Rahner, K. (1984). *The Practice of Faith: A Handbook of Contemporary Spirituality*. First published by Crossroad Publishing Company.

8: Pope Francis. Quoted on The Jesuit Conference of Asia and the Pacific website. Retrieved from https://jcapsj.org/the-buddha-jesus/.

Part three – Towards a Universal Understanding
Chapter 1: Towards the Universal within Western Christianity

1: Darwin, C. (1879). Letter no. 12041. *Darwin Correspondence*

Project. Retrieved from http://www.darwinproject.ac.uk/DCP-LETT-12041.

2: Teilhard de Chardin, P. Quoted in Delio, I. (2013). *The Unbearable Wholeness of Being: God, Evolution, and the Power of Love.* Orbis Books.

3: MacGregor, D. (2020). *Christianity Expanding - Into Universal Spirituality.* John Hunt Publishing.

4: Einstein, A. (1950). Letter quoted in *The New York Times* (29 March 1972) and *The New York Post* (28 November 1972).

5: MacGregor, D. (2020). *Christianity Expanding - Into Universal Spirituality.* John Hunt Publishing.

6: Currivan, J. (2017). *The Cosmic Hologram: In-formation at the Center of Creation.* Inner Traditions.

7: Psalm 8. *New King James Version.*

8: McPhee, J. (1981). *Basin and Range.* Farrar, Straus & Giroux.

9: International Association For Near-Death Studies, Inc. Retrieved from https://iands.org.

Chapter 3: Influences on Christian Thought Beyond the World of Science

1: Larsen, J. B. (2007, October 31). Globalization: A Rendezvous with Reality. *Huffington Post.*

2: Tutu, Archbishop Desmond. Interview with Maui Media. Retrieved from https://mauimedia.com/godhasadream/q-and-a-with-desmond-tutu-about-god-has-a-dream/.

3: Pennington, Fr. Basil. Retrieved from
https://www.contemplativeoutreach.org/2020/06/19/a-borderless-practice-the-interspiritual-invitation-of-centering-prayer/.

Chapter 4: Evolving Christianity – key features

1: Tickle, P. (2008). *The Great Emergence: How Christianity is Changing and why.* Baker Books. Also, (2021). *Emergence Christianity: What it is, where it is going and why it matters.* Baker Books.

2: Finley, J. The Alternative Orthodoxy is the orthodoxy of the intimacy of love that breaks our heart open to see how unexplainably precious we are.

3: Rohr, R. (2019). Introduction. Oneing, The Universal Christ, Volume 8, Number 1, Spring 2019. Copyright © 2019 by CAC. All rights reserved worldwide.

4.Ibid

5.Ibid

6: Ephesians 1:10. *New Revised Standard Version.*

7: Rohr, R. (2019). Introduction. In Oneing, The Universal Christ, Volume 8, Number 1, Spring 2019. Copyright © 2019 by CAC. All rights reserved worldwide.

8: Redfield, W. (2013). Sermon. Retrieved from
https://www.williamredfield.com/writings/2018/6/24/what-is-wisdom.

9: Ibid.

10: Borg, M. J. Retrieved from https://marcusjborg.org/quotes/.

11: Retrieved from https://www.irest.org/nonduality-and-irest.

12: Barnhart, Fr B. (1999). *Second Simplicity.* Paulist Press.

13: Bourgeault, Cynthia. (2015). Jesus Christ: Weekly Summary (2015-03-28). Retrieved from https://cac.org/daily-meditations/jesus-christ-weekly-summary-2015-03-28.

14: Bourgeault, Cynthia. (2007). *Christophany: Experiencing the Fullness of Christianity.* The Contemplative Society. Available at: https://www.contemplative.org/product/christophany-experiencing-the-fullness-of-christianity-1/

14: Rohr, R. (2015, March 28). Daily Meditations. Retrieved from Richard Rohr's Daily Meditations.

15: Borg, M. J. (n.d.). *The God We Never Knew.* Retrieved from The Marcus J Borg Foundation.

16: . HeartMath Institute. (n.d.). Research. Retrieved from HeartMath Institute Research.

17: Hillman, A. (2008). *Awakening the Energies of Love: Fire for the Second Time.* Quoted on Anne Hillman's website. Retrieved from annehillman.net.

18: Rossi, V. (n.d.). *Sacred Cosmology in the Christian Tradition. Orthodox Fellowship of the Transfiguration.* Retrieved from Orthodox Fellowship of the Transfiguration.

19: O'Murchu, D. (2017). *Incarnation: A New Evolutionary Threshold.* Orbis Books.

20: The King Center. (n.d.). *The King Philosophy.* Retrieved from The King Center.

21: Pagels, E. (2006). *The Gnostic Gospels.* Weidenfeld & Nicolson.

22: Mobsby, I., & Berry, M. (2014). *A New Monastic Handbook: From Vision to Practice.* Canterbury Press.

Part four – The Emerging Future

Chapter 1: Beyond Christianity – the challenge and opportunity of Contemporary Spiritual Movements

1: Johnson, K., & Ord, D. R. (n.d.). *A Spirituality for the 21st Century: Inevitabilities and Possibilities.* Retrieved from Kosmos Journal.

2: Sheldrake, R. (2017). *Science and Spiritual Practices: Reconnecting through direct experience.* Coronet Books. Also, Sheldrake, R. (2019). *Ways to Go Beyond and Why they Work: Seven Spiritual Practices in a Scientific Age.* Coronet.

3: *The New King James Version.* (1982). John 3:8. Nashville: Thomas Nelson.

4: *Resurgence & Ecologist* Magazine. (n.d.). Retrieved from Resurgence.

Positive News. (n.d.). Retrieved from Positive News.

Caduceus Magazine. (n.d.). Retrieved from Caduceus.

Chapter 2: A Relevant Spirituality

1: Kumar, N. N. (n.d.) *Does Religion Have a Place in the 21st Century?* Available at:

https://www.fairobserver.com/culture/does-religion-have-a-

□

place-in-the-century-43495/

2: *The Holy Bible: New King James Version.* (1982) Nashville: Thomas Nelson.

3: The Quiet Garden Movement. (n.d.) Available at: https://quietgarden.org

4: Caddy, E. (2007) *Opening Doors Within.* Findhorn: Findhorn Press.

5: Bourgeault, C. (2010) *The Meaning of Mary Magdalene: Discovering the Woman at the Heart of Christianity.* Boston, MA: Shambhala Publications.

6: *The Holy Bible: King James Version.* (1611) London: Robert Barker.

7: Pope Francis. (2015) *Laudato Si.* Vatican City: Libreria Editrice Vaticana.

8: WYSE International. (n.d.) Available at: https://www.wyse-ngo.org

9: Johnson, K., and Ord, D.R. (n.d.) *A Spirituality for the 21st Century: Inevitabilities and Possibilities.* Available at: https://www.kosmosjournal.org/article/a-spirituality-for-the-21st-century-inevitabilities-and-possibilities/

10: Scientific and Medical Network. (n.d.) Available at: https://scientificandmedical.net

11: Schweitzer, A. (n.d.) *Reverence for Life.* Available at: https://en.wikipedia.org/wiki/Reverence_for_Life

12: *The Holy Bible: New King James Version.* (1982) Psalm 82:6. Nashville: Thomas Nelson.

13: Trevelyan, G. (n.d.) *We are all droplets of divinity*. Available at: https://www.sirgeorgetrevelyan.org.uk

14: *The Holy Bible: New King James Version*. (1982) John 14:12. Nashville: Thomas Nelson.

15: Baring, A. (2015) *Dream of the Cosmos: A Quest for the Soul*. Wilton: Archive Publishing.

Chapter 3: Embodying a Loving Universal Perspective – A reflection

1: Teilhard de Chardin, P. (1973) *Toward the Future*. [Original work published 1936].

2: Rumi, J., translated by Barks, C. (n.d.) *A Great Wagon*.

3: Costley, Rev Daniel, Unitarian Minister, from a newsletter

4: Ibid.

Postscript:

1: Berry, T. (1988) *The Dream of the Earth*. San Francisco: Sierra Club Books.

2: Delio, I. (2015) *Making All Things New: Catholicity, Cosmology, Consciousness*. New York: Orbis Books.

SLEEPY LION

P U B L I S H I N G

If you are interested in publishing, writing and you love to read, then head over to www.sleepylionpublishing.com

Otherwise, all questions can be sent to enquiries@sleepylionpublishing.com

If you would like to submit any work, whether a manuscript, short story, article, blog post or even artwork, then send us an email at submissions@sleepylionpublishing.com

We offer different paid contracts on smaller pieces, so whether you would rather an upfront payment, or to make money over time, we also personalize our collaborations. So, get in contact now and start earning money from your work!

https://www.facebook.com/sleepylionpublishing/

On our website you will find:

-Our personal editing, illustrating and publishing services and traditional royalty contracts

- Blog posts

 -Articles on writing and reading

-Essays

-Short Stories

-Poetry

-And much, much more...